Knitted & Crocheted
Slippers

ALISON HOWARD

Knitted & Crocheted
Slippers

For Melanie Jonker in Queensland, Australia
(melsnattyknits), and all the other bloggers who have said
nice things about my designs. Keep on blogging!

First published 2014 by

Guild of Master Craftsman Publications Ltd
Castle Place, 166 High Street, Lewes,
East Sussex BN7 1XU

Text © Alison Howard, 2014
Copyright in the Work © GMC Publications Ltd, 2014

ISBN 978 1 86108 982 3

Whilst every effort has been made to obtain permission
from the copyright holders for all material used in this
book, the publishers will be pleased to hear from anyone
who has not been appropriately acknowledged and to
make the correction in future reprints.

The publishers and author can accept no legal
responsibility for any consequences arising from the
application of information, advice or instructions given
in this publication.

A catalogue record for this book is available from the
British Library.

Publisher Jonathan Bailey
Production Manager Jim Bulley
Managing Editor Gerrie Purcell
Pattern checking Jude Roust
Senior Project Editors Sara Harper and Cath Senker
Editor Nicola Hodgson
Managing Art Editor Gilda Pacitti
Designer Ginny Zeal
Photographers Anthony Bailey and Andrew Perris

Set in Gill Sans
Colour origination by GMC Reprographics
Printed and bound in China

Why we love slippers

EVERYBODY NEEDS SLIPPERS. THERE'S NOTHING NICER THAN coming in after a busy day to find a snuggly pair waiting for you. Kicking off your outdoor shoes and wriggling your toes into your favourite slippers is just like giving your tired toes a hug.

There's one problem: the shops only seem to stock a range of slippers at one time of the year. If yours are looking sloppy and shabby and you just can't buy any more, why not try making your own? If you've never tried making slippers, it's not as difficult as you might think. Fabric produced from yarn stretches to give a good fit, so you can produce great results whatever your level of skill. Making your own slippers means you can match your favourite PJs or dressing-gown, or just use up oddments from your stash.

This book features designs for knitters of all abilities, from the novice to the more confident crafter, plus a few simple crochet numbers that use only the basic stitches. Whether you need a chunky style to ward off winter chills or a daintier design for warmer weather, there is something to fit the bill. There are various ways of adding soles to make your creations non-slip and more durable. So grab a ball of yarn, pick your favourite design and prepare to give those feet a treat.

"A slipper is for life, not just for the winter..."

Contents

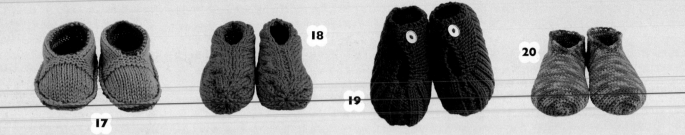

25

26

27

28

29

30

The easiest possible slippers are made from a T-shape of knitting and can be made in any size. Even a new knitter who has only mastered casting on, casting off and garter stitch can produce impressive results.

It's a wrap!

Size

To fit any size foot

Tension

24 sts and 48 rows to 4in (10cm) measured over garter stitch (unstretched) using 3.5–4mm needles. Use larger or smaller needles if necessary to obtain the correct tension.

Note: *Yarn thickness varies widely according to brand, so be sure to work a tension square first (see page 133).*

Materials

1–2 x 50g balls DK yarn
Pair of 3.5mm (UK–:US4) or 4mm (UK8:US6) knitting needles
Darning needle
Large sewing needle
Two or four buttons, depending on size made

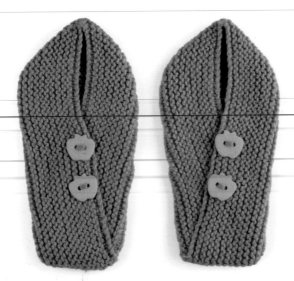

Special abbreviations

Sl1: slip the first stitch of the row to the working needle without knitting it.

First things first

Before starting to knit, you need to know three things:

A) How many stitches to cast on for the upper.

B) How many stitches you need for the sole.

C) How many stitches to cast off on each side.

Here's how to do it

Measure the length of the foot in inches, or refer to the size guide (see page 132). Measure the width of the instep in inches under the arch of the foot. A child's instep should be 2–2.5in, a woman's 2.5–3in and a man's 3–4in.

What to do next

Use the chart below, which gives a range of sizes based on average measurements. For a custom fit, follow the instructions below.

A) Double the foot length measurement and multiply by 6 (or the number of stitches produced per inch if using a different yarn). For a 9in (23cm) foot with a 3in (7.5cm) sole worked in DK yarn this is $9 + 9 \times 6 = 108$.

B) Multiply the instep measurement in inches by 6 (or the number of stitches produced per inch if using a different yarn) and subtract from the number of upper stitches. For the example, this is $108 - 18 = 90$.

C) Halve the result.

Slipper (make 2)

Using the cable cast-on method (see page 136), cast on the number of stitches given on the chart or calculated according to your measurements (**A**).

Number of stitches required

Foot length (inches)	No. of stitches to cast on	Suggested heel width	Rows to work before heel	No. of heel stitches	Stitches to cast off on either side
4	48	1½in	18	10	20
5	60	1¾in	22	10	25
6	72	2in	24	12	30
7	84	2½in	28	14	35
8	96	2¾in	32	16	40
9	108	3in	36	18	45
10	120	3½in	40	20	50
11	132	3¾in	44	22	55
12	144	4in	48	24	60

Pattern row: Sl1, knit every stitch to the end of the row.

Rep until piece measures approximately the same as the instep width.

Next row: cast off the number of stitches calculated at **C**.

Next row: as previous row (you should be left with the number of sole stitches calculated at **B**).

Working on these stitches only, repeat pattern row until sole measures same as foot length when stretched slightly. Cast off (see page 137), leaving a long end.

Making up

Do not press the work as this will flatten the garter stitch and ruin its elasticity. Lay out the pieces WS up; the cast-on edge has a distinctive appearance on the right side and this is intended to show when the slipper is wrapped.

Right slipper

Pin right corner of cast-on edge to left corner of cast-off edge and sew

together through the edges. Pin left corner of cast-on edge to right corner of cast-off edge and oversew across, using the long yarn end left when casting off. Sew the side seams through the edges of the rows, keeping seams as flat as possible. Try on the slipper to work out the position of the buttons; the top button should be about halfway up the slipper when it is folded flat. Sew on the buttons to keep the wrap in place, using two buttons for the larger sizes. Catch the wrap of the slipper in place when you are happy with the position of the buttons.

Left slipper

Complete as for the right slipper, reversing the direction of the wrap.

Adding soles

See page 134 for ideas on adding non-slip soles to the slippers.

Variations

- Make the slippers in exactly the same way, but in 1 × 1 rib (see page 140).

- Use a contrasting shade for the sole section; it is ideal for using up oddments of yarn.

- Make the slippers in finer or thicker yarn. See page 133 for a chart of yarns and suggested tensions. Aran-weight yarn should give a tension of 5 to 5.5 sts to 1in (2.5cm) in width over garter stitch using 4–4.5mm needles. Make sure that you adjust the number of stitches per inch (2.5cm) when calculating how many stitches to cast on and cast off.

Tip

It is easy to count rows in garter stitch: one ridge equals two rows.

These really easy slippers are made from one big square and four small squares sewn together. They can be made in any size, and in any weight of yarn, so they are great for using up odds and ends of leftover yarn.

Simple squares

Size
To fit any size foot

Tension
DK: 24 sts to 4in (10cm) in width, measured over garter stitch using size 3.5mm needles.
Aran: 20 sts to 4in (10cm) in width, measured over garter stitch using size 4mm needles.
Chunky: 16 sts to 4in (10cm) in width, measured over garter stitch using size 4.5mm needles.

Use larger or smaller needles if necessary to obtain the correct tension.

Materials
Oddments of yarn of a similar composition
Darning needle

Note: If you want to make the large squares in a single colour you will need 1 x 50g ball of DK, 2 x 50g balls of Aran or 3 x 50g balls of Chunky yarn in this shade.

Measuring

Measure the length of the foot. Don't add anything for luck, as garter stitch is very stretchy. If your grasp of Pythagoras' theorem (handy for working out the diagonal of a square) is rusty, see the chart below left. If your foot is between two sizes, go slightly smaller.

The diagonal of each big square, slightly stretched, should be the same length as the foot. One point goes at the toe, the opposite point at the heel, and the two remaining points wrap around to join across the instep. Each little square should be a quarter the size of a big square. Two of these are used for the heel and toe, and two to fill the instep.

Planning your squares

Size	Foot length	Side of big square	Diagonal (approx)	Side of small square	Diagonal (approx)
Child XS (UK 5–6)	4–5½in (10–14cm)	3in (7.5cm)	4¼in (10.6cm)	1½in (3.75cm)	2⅛in (5.3cm)
Child S (UK 7–8)	5½–6in (14–15cm)	3½in (9cm)	5in (12.5cm)	1¾in (4.5cm)	2½in (6.4cm)
Child M (UK 8–9)	6–6½in (15–16.5cm)	4in (10cm)	5⅗in (14.15cm)	2in (5cm)	2⅘in (7cm)
Child L (UK 10–12)	6½–7in (16.5–17.75cm)	4½in (11cm)	6⅖in (16.25cm)	2½in (5.5cm)	3½in (8cm)
Child XL (UK 1–2)	7–8in (17.75–20cm)	5in (12.5cm)	7in (17.75cm)	2½in (6.25cm)	3½in (8.8cm)
Adult XS (UK 3–4)	8–8½in (20–21.5cm)	5½in (14cm)	7⅘in (19.75cm)	2¾in (7cm)	3⁹⁄₁₀in (9.9cm)
Adult S (UK 4–5)	8½–9½in (21.5–24cm)	6in (15cm)	8½in (21.5cm)	3in (7.5cm)	4¼in (10.6cm)
Adult M (UK 6–7)	9½–10in (24–25cm)	6½in (16.5cm)	9⅕in (23.3cm)	3¼in (8.25cm)	4⅗in (11.6cm)
Adult L (UK 8–9.5)	10–10½in (25–26.5cm)	7in (17.75cm)	9⁹⁄₁₀in (25cm)	3½in (9cm)	5in (12.5cm)
Adult XL (UK 10–12)	11½–12½in (29–31.75cm)	8in (20cm)	11³⁄₁₀in (28.25cm)	4in (10cm)	5⅗in (14.15cm)

Big squares (make 2)

Cast on 3 sts.

Row 1: Knit.

Row 2: Inc by knitting into front and back of next stitch, k to end (4 sts).

Rep row 2 until the side of the square measures half the foot length and there is an even number of stitches on the needle. Note the number of stitches.

Next row: Knit.

Dec row: K to last 3 sts, k2tog, k1.

Rep this row until there are 3 sts left on the needle.

Next row: K2tog, k1.

Cast off, leaving a long yarn end for sewing up.

Variations

- Make the squares using straight knitting, casting on enough stitches to achieve the measurement needed (see chart, right) and slipping the first stitch of every row.
- Omit the instep squares to produce a smaller, fold-up slipper that can easily be carried in a handbag or pocket.
- Make all the squares in a single colour and place them with the lines of garter stitch alternating for a basket-weave effect. Finish off with blanket stitch (see page 148) or by oversewing (see page 149).

Little squares (make 4 for each slipper)

Work as for the big squares until there are half as many stitches on the needle.

Next row: Knit across all sts.

Next row: K to last 3 sts, k2tog, k1. Rep this row until there are 3 sts on the needle.

Next row: K2tog, k1.

Cast off, leaving yarn end for sewing up.

Tip

Use up all your yarn oddments by working squares in random colours, joining in different shades if you run out before the end.

Making up

Measure and mark the centre of each side of a big square. Place a toe square at one end and join to the big square, placing the points at the centre of the sides. Repeat this process with a heel square. Bring the two free points of the big square and the free point of the toe square together and join, then finish sewing up the toe. Open out the slipper and fill in the gaps in the instep with small squares set with one of the points downwards. Turn the slipper the right way out. Complete the second slipper to match. If preferred, catch down the free points of the instep squares using small stitches.

Chart for straight squares

Size	Cast on (DK)	Cast on (Aran)	Cast on (Chunky)
3in (7.5cm)	18	16	12
3½in (9cm)	22	18	14
4in (10cm)	24	20	16
4½in (11cm)	28	22	18
5in (12.5cm)	30	26	20
5½in (14cm)	34	28	22
6in (15cm)	36	30	24
6½in (16.5cm)	40	34	26
7in (17.75cm)	42	36	28
7½in (19cm)	46	38	30
8in (20cm)	48	40	32

This garter-stitch bootee has no complicated size variations
and only one set of instructions: just change the yarn and needles
to make slippers for all the youngsters in the family.

Easy peasy bootees

Sizes and materials

Up to 9 months: 1 × 50g ball 4ply; 3mm needles

Up to 18 months: 1 × 50g ball 4ply; 3.5mm needles

18–24 months: 1 × 50g ball DK; 3.5mm needles

Shoe size 6–7: 1 × 50g ball DK; 4mm needles

Shoe size 8–9: 2 × 50g balls DK; 5mm needles

Shoe size 10–11: 1 × 100g ball Aran; 4.5mm needles

Shoe size 12–13: 1 × 100g ball Aran; 5mm needles

Shoe size 1–2: 2 × 50g balls Chunky; 5.5mm needles

Shoe size 3–4: 2 × 50g balls Chunky; 6mm needles

Shoe size 5–6: 2–3 × 50g balls Chunky; 6.5mm needles

Note: *For UK/US shoe size conversion chart see page 132.*

Stitch holder or spare needle

Darning needle

Eyelets (optional): K2, (yf, k2tog); rep instruction in brackets across row.

Next: Work 5 rows in garter stitch, ending with RS row so WS of the work is facing to begin the instep shaping. This means the best side of the cast-on edge will be on show when the cuff is turned down. There should be three visible ridges of garter stitch.

Shape instep

Next row (WS): K23, turn, leaving rem 11 sts on a holder or spare needle.

Next row: K12, turn, leaving rem 11 sts on a stitch holder or spare needle. Work 24 rows of garter stitch on the centre 12 sts, which will give you 12 ridges. Break off yarn.

Shape foot

With the right side of work facing, slip the first 11 sts (which have already been worked) back onto the right (working) needle. Rejoin the yarn.

Next row: Pick up and knit 11 sts along the right side of the instep, working into the first two strands of the ends of the first 11 garter-stitch ridges. Knit across the 12 centre sts. Pick up and knit 11 sts down the left side of the instep, working into the ends of the garter-stitch ridges. Knit to end. There should be 56 sts on your needle.

Tension

Garter stitch can be stretched to accommodate a range of sizes, so is ideal for making slippers. This is a guide to the number of stitches that will be produced over 4in (10cm) in width:

Yarn weight	Needles	Stitches to 4in (10cm) in width
4ply	3mm	28
4ply	3.25–3.5mm	26
DK	4mm	24
DK	4.5mm	22
Aran	4.5mm	20
Aran	5mm	18
Chunky	5.5mm	16
Chunky	6mm	15
Chunky	6.5mm	14
Chunky	7mm	13

Special abbreviations

Yf: yarn forward (creates a 'hole' in the knitting; used here to make eyelets).

Note: The examples were worked using Patons Fairytale Colour 4 Me 4ply in pale green; Lang Omega DK in pale pink; Adriafil Navy Cotton Chunky in rose pink (size 1–2) and pale green (size 3–4), and Artesano British Wool Chunky in pink (size 5–6).

Slipper (make 2)

Cast on 34 sts loosely and work 20 rows of k1, p1 rib (single rib; see page 140). If you want to add a tie to your slippers, work the last row as the eyelet row below. To ensure a close fit, you may want to work the ribbing using needles one size smaller, but cast on using the specified size so the slipper is easy to put on and take off.

Next: Work 9 rows in garter stitch (5 ridges). The stitches will be closely packed and quite tricky to work at first, but this will become easier.

Shape heel
Row 1: K1, k2tog, k to last 3 sts, k2tog, k1 (54 sts).
Rows 2 and 4: K all sts.
Row 3: As row 1 (52 sts).

Shape toe
Row 1: K1, k2tog, k19; (k2tog) 4 times, k to last 3 sts, k2tog, k1 (46 sts).
Row 2: Knit.
Cast off, leaving a long yarn end for sewing up.

Making up
Fold the slipper in half, RS out and, using the long end left when casting off, join the foot seam so that it lies as flat as possible. To do this, pick up one strand of the first cast-off stitch, then take the yarn across and pick up one strand of the last cast-off stitch. Repeat with the second stitches and continue in this way along the row. Fasten off securely and darn the end back along the row, taking care not to gather your work. Now turn the slipper inside out and, using the long yarn end left when casting on, join the ribbing to just over halfway down using mattress stitch (see page 147). Turn work the right way out

and join the rest of the ribbing, then join the garter-stitch section following the instructions for garter-stitch joins (see page 147). Darn in all ends.

Adding soles
Suitable non-slip soles can be made by cutting out a foot shape from chamois leather, suede or faux suede and sewing to the bottom of the slipper. (For more information on adding soles, see page 134.)

Ties
Add ribbon or make ties by plaiting strands of toning or contrasting yarn, knotting the ends and trimming to form a tassel. Use three strands for smaller sizes and six for larger sizes. A length of I-cord (see page 151) or a crocheted chain (see page 144) may also be used.

Tip
If the picked-up stitches are not as neat as you would like, don't worry – just tidy up any holes by oversewing from the reverse side of your work using matching yarn.

This ankle-warming design, worked sideways in easy garter stitch,
is ideal for an inexperienced knitter who is keen to move up a notch.
Simple short-row shaping with no wrapped stitches gives a fabulous fit.

Sideways slouch

Size

To fit any size foot

Tension

13 sts and 26 rows to 4in (10cm) measured over garter stitch
using 6mm needles. Use larger or smaller needles if necessary
to obtain the correct tension.

Materials

Artesano British Wool Chunky, 100% wool
(115yds/105m per 100g)
2[2:3:3:3] × 100g skeins 05 Brown
Pair of 6mm (UK4:US10) knitting needles
Darning needle

Size chart

Size	UK adult size	European size	Length (in)	Length (cm)	Leg height (in)	Leg height (cm)
A	4–5	37–38	8–9	22	11	28
B	5–6	38–39	9–9½	23–24	11¾	30
C	6–7.5	40–41	9½–10	25–26	12½	32
D	7.5–8.5	42–43	10–10½	28	13¼	34
E	8.5–10	43–44	10½–11	30	14	36

Slipper (make 2)

Using 6mm needles and the cable cast-on method (see page 136), cast on 65[70:75:80:85] sts.

Calf shaping

Note: Slip the stitch after turning and pull yarn taut to prevent gaps in the work.

Row 1: Knit.
Row 2: K8, turn.
Row 3: Sl1, k to end of row.
Row 4: K16, turn.
Row 5: Sl1, k to end of row.
Row 6: K24, turn.
Row 7: Sl1, k to end of row.
Row 8: K32, turn.
Row 9: Sl1, k to end of row.

Begin short-row toe shaping

Note:: Every fourth row at the toe end will be a short row, i.e. turned 5 sts before the end.

Row 10 (short row): K to last 5 sts, turn.
Row 11: Sl1, k to end of row.
Row 12: K all sts, ending at toe.

Shape first side of heel

Count across the row from the toe end and mark st 25[30:35:40:45].

Note: Decreases fall on either side of this stitch on subsequent rows.

Row 13 (dec): K to 2 sts before marked st, k2tog, k marked st, skpo, k to end.
Row 14 (short row): K to 5 sts from end of row, turn.
Row 15 (dec): Sl1, k to 2 sts before marked st, k2tog, k marked st, skpo, k to end.
Row 16: K across all sts.
Row 17 (dec): K to 2 sts before marked st, k2tog, k marked st, skpo, k to end.
Row 18 (short row): K to 5 sts from end of row, turn.
Row 19 (dec): Sl1, k to 2 sts before marked st, k2tog, k marked st, skpo, k to end.
Row 20: K all sts.
Row 21 (dec): K to 2 sts before marked st, k2tog, k marked st, skpo, k to end (55[60:65:70:75] sts).

Work upper section*

Row 22 (short row): K to 5 sts from end of row, turn.
Row 23: Sl1, k to end of row.
Row 24: K all sts.
Row 25: K all sts.
Rep rows 22–25 3[4:4:5:5] times, then rows 22–24 once.*

Shape second side of heel

Count across row from toe end and mark st 25[30:35:40:45].

Row 1 (inc): K to marked st, M1, k marked st, M1, k to end.

Row 2 (short row): K to last 5 sts, turn.

Row 3 (inc): Sl1, k to marked st, M1, k marked st, M1, k to end.

Row 4: Knit.

Row 5 (inc): K to marked st, M1, k marked st, M1, k to end.

Row 6 (short row): K to last 5 sts, turn.

Row 7 (inc): Sl1, k to marked st, M1, k marked st, M1, k to end.

Row 8: Knit.

Row 9 (inc): K to marked st, M1, k marked st, M1, k to end (65[70:75:80:85] sts back on needle).

Next row (short row): K to last 5 sts, turn.

Next row: Sl1, k to end.

Next row: K32, turn.

Next row: Sl1, k1, k to end.

Next row: K24, turn.

Next row: Sl1, k to end.

Next row: K16, turn.

Next row: Sl1, k to end.

Next row: K8, turn.

Next row: Sl1, k to end.

Next row: Knit.

Cast off.

Making up

Join corners of toe end, then fold toe flat with the join in the centre and oversew edges together (see page 149). Join the slipper as far as the heel shaping by oversewing, keeping it as flat as possible. Pin the back seam, matching the 'steps', and sew down firmly. Darn in ends. Weave laces through work and over back seam, lining up tiny holes left by short-row shaping steps.

Adding soles

See page 134 for ideas on adding non-slip soles to the slippers.

These easy slippers are worked in half treble crochet, which produces
a stretchy but firm fabric. They can be customized to fit exactly,
and are given a pretty finishing touch with a jaunty flower.

Two-tone

Sizes

S[M:L] to fit UK adult shoe size 3–4[5–6:7–8]

Tension

These slippers are customized to fit exactly; therefore
achieving an exact tension is not essential.

Materials

Sirdar Snuggly Baby Bamboo DK, 80% bamboo, 20% wool
(104yds/95m per 50g)
1 × 50g ball 158 Rinky Dinky Pink (A)
1 × 50g ball 169 Light Blue (B)
3.5mm (UK9:USE-4) crochet hook
4mm (UK8:USG-6) crochet hook
Darning needle

Slipper (make 2)

Beginning at toe and using A and 4mm hook, make a ring.

Round 1: 2 ch (to represent first htr), 7 htr in ring, sl st to top of 2 ch to join (8 sts).

Round 2: 2 ch, 1 htr in same place, 2 htr in each htr to end, sl st to top of 2 ch (16 sts).

Round 3: 2 ch, 1 htr in same place, (1 htr in each of next 3 htr, 2 htr in next htr); rep to last 3 htr, 1 htr in each of next 3 htr, sl st to join (20 sts).

Round 4: 2 ch, 1 htr in same place, (1 htr in each of next 4 htr, 2 htr in next htr); rep to last 4 htr, 1 htr in each of next 4 htr, sl st to join (24 sts).

Round 5: 2 ch, 1 htr in each htr to end, sl st to join (24 sts).

Round 6: 2 ch, 1 htr in same place, (1 htr in each of next 5 htr, 2 htr in next htr); rep to last 5 htr, 1 htr in each of next 5 htr, sl st to join (28 sts).

Round 7: 2 ch, 1 htr in each htr to end, sl st to join (28 sts).

Round 8: 2 ch, 1 htr in same place, (1 htr in each of next 6 htr, 2 htr in next htr); rep to last 6 htr, 1 htr in each of next 6 htr, sl st to join (32 sts).

Round 9: 2 ch, 1 htr in each htr to end, sl st to join (32 sts).

Round 10: 2 ch, 1 htr in same place, (1 htr in each of next 7 htr, 2 htr in next htr); rep to last 7 htr, 1 htr in each of last 7 htr, sl st to join (36 sts).

Round 11: 2 ch, 1 htr in each htr to end, sl st to join (36 sts).

Rep round 11 until toe section measures 4[4½:5]in (10[11.5:12.5]cm). Break off A.

Lay the slipper toe piece flat with the join underneath the foot. Mark the 8 sts at the centre of the slipper; join in B to the next st and begin to work back and forth in rows.

Next row: 2 ch, 1 htr in each of next 27 htr, turn leaving centre 8 sts free.

Next row: 2 ch, 1 htr in each st to end (28 sts).

Rep last row until slipper measures approx 6¾[7½:8¼]in (17[19:21]cm) or approx 1in (2.5cm) less than length required.

Tip

Run loose threads along the length of a row and crochet over them to save a lot of sewing in of ends.

Variation

Work the heel in a contrast colour.

Next row: Sl st over first 10 sts, 2 ch, 1 htr in each of next 7 htr, turn. Work 2½in (6cm) on these 8 sts. Fasten off, but do not break off yarn. With a spare length of yarn, join the two heel side seams.

Edging

Using 3.5mm hook and beg at the back of the heel, work 2 rows of dc round upper, placing 1 dc in each st across heel and front opening and 1 dc in each row end down sides. Fasten off and weave in ends.

Each of these snug boots is made from four hexagon motifs worked in simple treble crochet stitches. It is the perfect portable project as well as being an excellent stash-buster.

Hexagons

Size
S[M:L] to fit UK adult shoe size 4–5[5–6:7–8]

Tension
One completed motif measures 5[5½:6]in (12.75[14:15]cm) across from point to point.

Materials
1 x 50g ball Aran yarn in main colour (A)
1 x 50g ball Aran yarn in first contrast colour (B)
Oddments of Aran yarn in second contrast colour (C)
5.5mm (UK5:USI-9) crochet hook
Darning needle

Motif for sole and sides (make 6)

All sizes

Using C, make 4 ch. Join with a sl st to make a ring, ensuring sts are not twisted.

Round 1: 3 ch (to represent first treble); 17 tr in ring, join with sl st to top of 3 ch (18 tr). Break yarn and join in B to any stitch.

Round 2: 3 ch, 1 tr in same place, *(2 tr in next st); rep from * to end, join with sl st to top of 3 ch (36 tr). Break off B and join in A to any stitch.

Round 3: 3 ch, 1 tr in same place, *(miss 2 tr, 5 tr in next space, miss 2 tr, 2 tr in next space); rep from * 4 times more, miss 2 tr, 5 tr in next space. Join with sl st to top of 3 ch. Fasten off.

Round 4: 1 ch, 1 dc in each tr to centre tr of 5 tr, 2 dc in centre tr of 5 tr. Join with a sl st to first ch.

Tip

You can save a lot of time sewing in by crocheting over the ends after joining in yarn.

Medium size only

Rep round 4 once.

Large size only

Rep round 4 twice.

Fasten off.

Motif for toes (make 2)

Work as for sole and sides motif but change colour sequence as follows: round 1 in colour A; round 2 in C; round 3 in B.

Making up

Place a toe hexagon on a body hexagon, WS together, and join round four of the six sides. Place the remaining two body hexagons together and join two of the six sides for the heel and underfoot seam. Match the end of the underfoot seam to the free point of the first body hexagon, then finish join from this point to the top of the foot. Repeat for the other side of the slipper. Darn in ends.

Variation

Make the hexagons in random colours to use up all your oddments of yarn.

If you like a nice cuppa, you'll love these really silly slippers made in the same way as an old-fashioned tea cozy. The cushiony sections make them really warm and soft underfoot.

Cozy slippers

Size

To fit UK adult shoe size 4–5[5–6:6–7:7–8]

Tension

22 sts and 30 rows to 4in (10cm) square measured over stocking stitch using 4mm needles. Use larger or smaller needles if necessary to obtain the correct tension.

Materials

100g cotton or cotton-mix DK yarn in main colour (M)
100g cotton or cotton-mix DK yarn in contrast (C)
Pair of 3.5mm (UK–:US4) knitting needles
Pair of 4mm (UK8:US6) knitting needles
Darning needle

Slipper (make 2)

Beginning at heel end, using 3.5mm needles and M, cast on 38 sts.

Work 2 rows in garter stitch.

Row 3: K1, (m1, k2) to last st, m1, k1 (57 sts).

Join in C and change to 4mm needles.

Row 4: Using a strand of each yarn held together, knit the first stitch. Pulling the yarn firmly but not too tightly across the back of the work, (k5M, k5C) to last 6 sts, k5M, k1 with both colours.

Row 5: P1 with a strand of each yarn, (p5M, p5C) to last 6 sts, p5M, p1 with both colours.

Rep last 2 rows until work measures 7[7½:8:8½]in (18[19:20:21]cm) or

Tip

Keep a rule handy as you knit and hold your work against it every few rows to check the width.

length required. After a few rows, measure work. Aim for a width of about 7in (18cm) for an average foot or 7½in (19cm) for a wider foot. Adjust if necessary by stranding yarn more loosely across the back. Do not worry if the rows already worked are tighter, as these will be at the heel end.

Shape toe

Row 1: Keeping colours as set, k1 with a strand of each yarn, (k3, k2tog) to last st, k1 with a strand of each yarn (46 sts).

Next row: Keeping colours as set, p1 with a strand of each yarn, p to last st, p1 with a strand of each yarn.

Next row: K1 with a strand of each yarn, (k2tog, k2) to last st, k1 with a strand of each yarn (35 sts).

Next row: Keeping colours as set, p1 with a strand of each yarn, p to last st, p1 with a strand of each yarn.

Next row: K1 with a strand of each yarn, (k1, k2tog) to last st, k1 with a strand of each yarn (24 sts).

Next row: Keeping colours as set, p1 with a strand of each yarn, p to last st, p1 with a strand of each yarn.

Variations

- For a thicker slipper, use Aran-weight yarn, following the same instructions but pulling the sections in a little more tightly to achieve the correct width.
- Work in garter stitch throughout for an even thicker slipper, carrying the yarn across the front of the work on alternate rows.
- Trim with ribbon roses for less of a tea cozy effect.

Next row: Keeping colours as set, k1 with a strand of each yarn, k2tog to last st, k1 with a strand of each yarn. Break off yarn, leaving a long end. Thread yarn on a darning needle and pass through all the rem sts. Fasten off securely.

Making up

Join front seam to about halfway up the slipper. Join heel seam (cast-on edge), easing in the last inch to avoid creating a point. Make two small pompons for each slipper (see page 151) and attach as shown.

Fashion-conscious kids will love these soft, fluffy slippers.
The design is worked in a single flat piece on two needles,
and they are really fast to make using chunky yarn.

Mary Janes

Sizes

To fit UK shoe size 1[2:3:4]; approx foot length 8[8¼:8½:8¾]
in (20[21:22:23]cm)

Tension

16 sts and 20 rows to 4in (10cm) measured over stocking
stitch using 5mm needles. Use larger or smaller needles if
necessary to obtain the correct tension.

Materials and equipment

Sirdar Babouska Light Brushed Chunky, 52% wool,
39% acrylic, 9% nylon (126yds/115m per 50g)
1 × 50g ball 104 Grey
Pair of 5mm (UK6:US8) knitting needles
Spare needle for casting off
4mm (UK8:USG-6) crochet hook
Stitch markers
Darning needle

Special abbreviations

Yf: yarn forward (creates a 'hole' in the knitting; used here to make buttonhole).

Slipper (make 2)

Before starting, wind off a small ball of yarn to work second side of upper.

Heel

Cast on 6 sts.

Row 1: Knit.

Row 2: Purl.

Row 3: K1, m1, k to last 2 sts, m1, k1 (8 sts).

Row 4: Purl.

Rep rows 3 and 4 until there are 16 sts on needle.

Mark beg and end of last row.

Cont in stocking stitch until work measures 5½[6¼:6½:6¾]in (14[16:16.5:17.25]cm) from beg, ending with a purl row.

Shape toe

Row 1: K1, skpo, k to last 3 sts, k2tog, k1 (14 sts).

Next row: Purl.

Rep last 2 rows until there are 6 sts on needle. Mark both sides of this row for end of toe.

Shape upper

Row 1: K1, m1, k to last 2 sts, m1, k1 (8 sts).

Row 2: Purl.

Rep last 2 rows until there are 16 sts on needle.

Work in st st for 3¼[3½:3¾:4]in (8.5[9:9.5:10]cm) from toe markers, ending with a purl row.

Shape sides

K6, join in small ball of yarn and cast off 4 sts, k to end.

Both sides of the slipper are now on one needle and will be worked one after the other to ensure that each side is exactly the same length.

Next row: P sts on both needles, remembering to change balls of yarn.

Next row: K4, k2tog on first needle; skpo, k4 on second needle (5 sts on each needle).

Beg and ending with a purl row, work in stocking stitch until sides reach the first set of markers when slipper is folded at toe.

Next row: K1, m1, k to end on first needle; k to last st, m1, k1 on second needle (6 sts on each needle).

Work three rows in stocking stitch.

Next row: K1, m1, k to end on first needle; k to last st, m1, k1 on second needle (7 sts on each needle).

Work in stocking stitch until sides meet at centre of cast-on edge, ending with a purl row.*

Three-needle cast-off

Knit across first needle so one side is on each needle. Holding needles parallel with RS of work together, use a spare needle to knit together the first stitch from each needle. Rep, then pass first stitch over second stitch to cast off. Rep along row.

Note: *If you don't feel you can manage this just cast off all stitches at * and sew up the heel instead.*

Strap (make 2)

Cast on 4 sts.
Row 1: Knit.
Row 2: K1, p2, k1.
Rep last 2 rows until strap measures 3½[3½:3¾: 3¾]in (9[9:9.5:9.5]cm).

Buttonhole

K2tog, yf, k2.
Work 2 more rows.
Next row: Skpo, K2tog.
Cast off.

Making up

Join upper to sole along sides from the outside using mattress stitch (see page 147), working through just the very last stitch of each row. With RS facing, work a row of double crochet around the edge of the slipper. Sew on straps and attach buttons.

Tip

To add a sole, cut two strips of chamois leather 1in (2.5cm) less than the slipper's length and about 2½in (6cm) wide. Trim corners at an angle to follow toe and heel decreases. Attach to heel section before sewing up rest of the slipper.

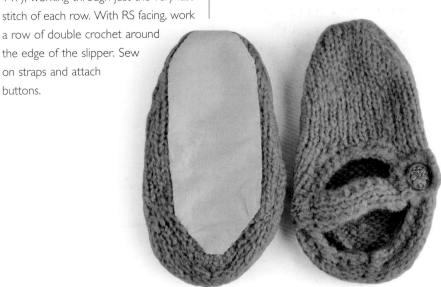

These ingenious slippers are quick and easy to make, but fit like a dream thanks to a stretchy slipped-stitch pattern. The chunky pure wool yarn will keep your toes as warm as toast all winter long.

Toasty toes

Size

S[M:L] to fit UK adult shoe size 3–4[5–6:7–8]

Tension

12 sts to 4in (10cm) in width, measured over pattern using 7mm needles. Use larger or smaller needles if necessary to obtain the correct tension.

Materials and equipment

Artesano British Wool Chunky, 100% machine-washable wool (115yds/105m per 100g)
1[1:2] × 100g hanks 04 Mushroom
Oddment of contrasting shade of same/similar yarn for edging
Pair of 7mm (UK2:US10.5) knitting needles
5.5mm (UK5:US1-9) crochet hook
Darning needle
Two ¾in (20mm) buttons or toggles (optional, for decoration)
Note: *Size M can be made with just one hank of the specified yarn if the edging is worked with an oddment of contrasting or toning Chunky yarn.*

Tip

If you have particularly wide feet, follow the instructions for the next size up but keep to the lengths given for your size.

Special abbreviations

Yb: yarn back.

Yf: yarn forward.

Note: *These techniques are used to make the slipped-stitch pattern; see below.*

Slipped-stitch pattern

Row 1: *K1, yf, sl1, yb; rep from * to last 2 sts, k1, yf, sl1.

Row 2: Purl.

Row 3: *Yf, sl1, yb, k1; rep from * to end.

Row 4: Purl.

Slipper (make 2)

Cuff and heel

Using 7mm needles and a cable cast-on (see page 136), cast on 44[48:52] sts. Work in pattern until piece measures 4½[5:5½]in (11[12:14]cm).

Next row: Cast off 9[10:11] sts loosely, patt to end.

Next row: Cast off 9[10:11] sts loosely, p to end (26[28:30] sts).

Foot section

Cont in patt until work measures 7[8:9] in (18[20:22.5]cm).

Shape toe

Row 1: Skpo, patt to last 2 sts, k2tog.

Row 2: Purl.

Rep these 2 rows, dec I st at each end of every alt row, until there are I4[I6:I8] sts on needles.
Break off yarn leaving a long end, thread on a darning needle and run through rem sts. Pull tight and fasten off securely.

Making up

Fold work widthways and join the two ends of the cast-on row from RS, making sure work lies flat. Sew two-thirds of the way along row, then run yarn through the remaining stitches and gather slightly before completing the seam, to avoid creating an obvious point at the heel. Fasten off and weave in end. Using the length of yarn left when casting off and working upwards from the toe, join seam as far as the point where the stitches were cast off on each side. Fasten off securely, taking yarn across several times to create a bar on which to attach the rosette.

Edging

Row I: Using contrast yarn, 5.5mm crochet hook and with WS facing, work a row of dc all around edge, placing I dc in each of the row ends, 2 dc in each corner and I dc in every other st along top edge. Turn.
Row 2: I dc in first dc, (3 ch, miss I dc, I dc in next dc) to end. Fasten off.

Rosette (make 2)

Using contrasting yarn, make a large loop round three fingers and work (Idc, 4ch) six times into loop. Draw loop up tightly and fasten off. Attach to front of slipper.

Variations

- The reverse side of this pattern is just as attractive, so use whichever side you prefer.
- For a plainer effect, work two rows of double crochet for the edging in the same yarn as used for the slipper.

Tweedy yarn makes a snug-fitting slipper with a traditional look that is ideal for either gender. These slippers are worked on two needles with easy shaping, and make a good project for a novice knitter.

Chunky tweed

Sizes

S[M:L] to fit UK adult shoe size 4–5.5[6–7.5:8–10]

Tension

13 sts and 22 rows to 4in (10cm) measured over stocking stitch using 5.5mm needles. Use larger or smaller needles if necessary to obtain the correct tension.

Materials and equipment

Debbie Bliss Winter Garden Chunky, 30% llama, 30% wool, 20% silk, 20% linen (108yds/100m per 100g)
1 x 100g skein 02 Autumn Leaf (M)
Wendy Mode Chunky, 50% merino wool, 50% acrylic (151yds/140m per 100g)
1 x 100g ball 220 Coal (C)
Pair of 5mm (UK6:US8) knitting needles
Pair of 5.5mm (UK5:US9) knitting needles
Darning needle

KNITTED & CROCHETED SLIPPERS

Slipper (make 2)
Sole
Using 5.5mm needles and C, cast on 45[51:57] sts.

Row 1: K, placing a marker on the centre stitch.

Row 2: K1, m1, k to marked stitch, m1, k1, m1, k to last st, m1, k1 (49[55:61] sts).

Row 3 and alternate rows: Knit.

Row 4: As row 2 (53[59:65] sts).
Rep last 2 rows until there are 69[75:81] sts on the needle.
Break off C and join in M.

Upper
Row 1: Knit.

Row 2: Purl.

Row 3: K23[26:29], ssk twice, k3tog, K9, sssk, k2tog twice, k to end (61[67:73] sts).

Row 4: Purl.

Tip
The quantities given should be enough to produce two pairs of slippers.

Row 5: K19[22:25], ssk twice, k3tog, K9, sssk, k2tog twice, k to end (53[59:65] sts).

Row 6: Purl.

Row 7: K31[34:37], ssk, turn.

Row 8: S11, p9, p2tog, turn.

Row 9: S11, k9, ssk, turn.

Row 10: S11, p9, p2tog, turn.
Rep last 2 rows until there are 37[39:41] sts on the needle.

Next row: S11, k9, ssk but do not turn; k to end (36[38:40] sts).

Next row: P to gap, p2tog across gap, purl to end (35[37:39] sts).

Next row: K across.

Next row: Purl.
Rep last two rows once.
Break off M and join in C.

Cuff
Change to 5mm needles and work 4 rows in garter stitch.
Cast off loosely using 5.5mm needles.

Making up
Join sole using end left when casting on.
Darn in yarn ends.

Luxurious and super-warm alpaca and wool yarn is ideal for this snug winter slipper that you'll never want to take off. A herringbone cable pattern adds interest to the toe.

Short and sweet

Size

S[M:L] to fit UK adult shoe size 4–5[5.5–6.5:7–8]; approx foot length 8½[9½:10½]in (22[24:27]cm)

Tension

17 sts and 21 rows to 4in (10cm) measured over stocking stitch on 4.5mm needles. Use larger or smaller needles if necessary to obtain the correct tension.

Materials and equipment

Artesano Aran, 50% superfine alpaca, 50% Peruvian highland wool (144yds/132m per 100g)

2 × 100g skeins 8316 Teal

Pair of 4.5mm (UK7:US7) knitting needles

Cable needle

Darning needle

Special abbreviations

C4B: slip next two stitches to cable needle and hold at back of work; k2 then knit stitches from cable needle.

C4F: slip next two stitches to cable needle and hold at front of work; k2 then knit stitches from cable needle.

Tip

There is room for socks inside these slippers; if you are unsure which size to work, choose the smaller size.

Herringbone cable pattern (worked over centre 13 sts)

Row 1: P2, C4B, k1, C4F, p2.
Row 2: K2, p9, k2.
Row 3: P2, k9, p2.
Row 4: As row 2.

Slipper (make 2)

Using 4.5mm needles, cast on 49[53:57] sts, leaving a long end for sewing up.
Work 6 rows in p1, k1 rib.

First series of increases

Row 1: K17[19:21], m1, k1, patt 13 sts, k1, m1, k17[19:21] (51[55:59] sts).

Row 2: P19[21:23], patt 13 sts, p19[21:23].
Row 3: K18[20:22], m1, k1, patt 13 sts, k1, m1, k18[20:22] (53[57:61] sts).
Row 4: P20[22:24], patt 13 sts, p20[22:24].
Row 5: K19[21:23], m1, k1, patt 13 sts, k1, m1, k19[21:23] (55[59:63] sts).
Row 6: P21[23:25], patt 13 sts, p21[23:25].

Cont thus, inc 2 sts on every alt row and working the additional sts in stocking stitch. At the same time, work patt (see above) over centre 13 sts until there are 61[65:69] sts in total on needle.

Next row: Beg in purl, work across in patt as set without increasing.
Now begin to inc 2 sts on every row thus:

Second series of increases

Row 1: K23[25:27], m1, k1, patt 13 sts, k1, m1, k23[25:27] (63[67:71] sts).
Row 2: P24[26:28], m1p, p1, patt 13 sts, p1, m1p, p24[26:28] (65[69:73] sts).
Cont thus, inc 2 sts on every row and working additional sts as stocking stitch, until there are 79[87:97] sts on needle. Work 6 rows in garter stitch without increasing.

Next: Cast off 1 st at beg of each of the next 8 rows (71[79:89] sts).
Cast off loosely, leaving a long end for sewing up.

Variations

- For a snug fit, run a circle of elastic through rib before closing last section.
- Make a deeper cuff by working extra rows of rib before beginning the pattern.
- Work the centre panel in garter stitch only for a simpler effect.

Making up

Join seam under foot and at centre back, ensuring that seam lies flat. Fold ribbing in half and stitch down on RS.

Adding soles

See page 134 for ideas on adding non-slip soles to the slippers.

Wear your favourite flip-flops (thongs) all year round by adding these clever geisha-style slipper socks. Worked on two needles, they're also perfect for taking on camping holidays.

Geisha

Size

S[M:L] to fit UK adult shoe sizes 4–5[5–6:7–8] or larger if required

Tension

22 sts and 30 rows to 4in (10cm) measured over stocking stitch using 4mm needles. Use larger or smaller needles if necessary to obtain the correct tension.

Materials and equipment

Artesano Superwash Merino, 100% machine-washable wool (122yds/112m per 50g)

2 x 50g balls 1291 Sea Blue

Pair of 4mm (UK8:US6) knitting needles

Spare needle for casting off

Darning needle

Special abbreviations

Tbl: through the back loops.

W&T (wrap and turn):

Knitwise = yarn forward, slip next st to
RH needle, yarn back, slip wrapped
stitch back to LH needle, turn.
Purlwise = yarn back, slip next stitch to
RH needle, yarn forward, slip wrapped
stitch back to LH needle, turn.

Right slipper

Using 4mm needles, cast on 48 sts and
work 2 rows in stocking stitch.
Work 8 rows in k1, p1 rib.
Work in stocking stitch for 3in (7.5cm).

Heel shaping

Row 1: K24, W&T.
Row 2: P23, W&T.
Row 3: K22, W&T.
Row 4: P21, W&T.

Cont working a stitch fewer between
wraps on every row, until the row 'K6,
W&T' has been worked.

Next row: P6, (pick up wrap, place on
needle, then purl wrap and next st
tog); rep to end.
Next row: K15, (pick up wrap, place
on needle, then knit wrap and next st
tog); rep until wrapped sts have been
worked off, then knit to end of row.
Work in stocking stitch for 5½[6½:7½]
in (14[16.5:19]cm) or length required
from curved end of heel (approx
2in/5cm less than foot length).

Divide for toe sections

Next row: K40, place last 8 sts on a
length of spare yarn, turn.
Next row: P32, place last 8 sts on a
length of spare yarn, turn.
Next row: Cast on 1 st, k to end, turn.

Next row: Cast on 1 st, p to end
(34 sts on needle).
Next row: K14, k2tog, k2, ssk, k14
(32 sts on needle).
Next row: Purl.
Next row: K13, k2tog, k2, ssk, k13
(30 sts).
Next row: P12, p2togtbl, p2, p2tog,
p12 (28 sts).
Next row: K11, k2tog, k2, ssk, k11
(26 sts).
Next row: P10, p2togtbl, p2, p2tog,
p10 (24 sts).
Next row: K9, k2tog, k2, ssk, k9
(22 sts).
Next row: P8, p2togtbl, p2, p2tog, p8
(20 sts).
Next row: K10, turn the work so RS
together and needles face same way.

Three needle cast-off

Hold needles parallel and, using a spare
needle, knit tog first stitch from each.
Rep with next stitch from each needle,
then cast off by taking the first stitch
over the second. Rep to end.
Fasten off, leaving a long yarn end
for sewing up.

Join four-toe section

Using the end left when casting off and
mattress stitch (see page 147), join
work down to where sts were left on
spare yarn.

Work big toe section

Rejoin yarn at the inside of the toe and replace the second group of 8 set-aside sts on the needle.

Row 1: Purl to end of row.

Row 2: K8, pick up and k 2 sts at the base of the four-toe section, then replace the first group of 8 set-aside sts on needle with the point inwards and knit across (18 sts).

Next row: Purl.

Work in stocking stitch until toe measures 1¼in (3cm) from base.

Next row: K1, ssk, k3, k2tog, k2, ssk, k3, k2tog, k1 (14 sts).

Next row: Purl.

Next row: K1, ssk, k1, k2tog, k2, ssk, k1, k2tog, k1 (10 sts).

Break yarn, leaving a long end for sewing up. Thread through rem sts and fasten off.

Left slipper

Work as for right slipper to heel shaping.

Tip

Working both slippers at the same time helps to ensure that row counts are the same and that sizes match.

Heel shaping

Row 1: Knit to last stitch, W&T.
Row 2: P23, W&T.
Row 3: K22, W&T.
Row 4: P21, W&T.

Cont in this way until the row 'K6, W&T' has been worked.

Next row: P6, (pick up wrap, place on needle, then purl wrap and next st tog); rep until all wrapped sts have been worked; p to end of row.

Next row: Knit, picking up and knitting together slipped sts and wraps.

Next row: Purl across.

Variation

If you are an experienced knitter, you can work this slipper in the round to avoid seams.

Cont in stocking stitch until work measures the same as right slipper from curve of heel or length required.

Completing left slipper

Work toe sections and make up as for right slipper.

This design is knitted in a single piece that looks odd until you sew it up, when it magically transforms into a cute slipper. Add a bit of hocus pocus with yarn and you can make it fit anyone from fairy to ogre.

Abracadabra

Size

To fit UK child shoe size 7–8 (approx age 2–3 years) up to UK adult shoe size 7–8 (any age)

Tension

Fine DK using 3mm needles: 24 sts to 4in (10cm) in width

Standard DK using 3.5mm needles: 22 sts to 4in (10cm) in width

Aran using 4mm needles: 20 sts to 4in (10cm) in width

Aran using 4.5mm needles: 18 sts to 4in (10cm) in width

Materials and equipment

Smallest size: 1 x 50g ball DK (example made using Bergère de France Barisienne DK)

Other sizes: 2 x 50g balls DK (example made using Artesano Superwash DK) or 1 x 100g ball Aran

Pair of 3mm, 4mm or 4.5mm knitting needles

Crochet hook in a similar size to knitting needles

Oddment of contrasting yarn for inner sole

Darning and sewing needles

Motifs, embroidered trim or ribbon to decorate

Tension note

For this design, tension length is not crucial because garter stitch is so stretchy, but widthways stitch count is important. Thickness of yarns can vary; DK is especially prone to variations. Check the tension carefully and never rely solely on the ball band.

Working out the size

Measure the length of the foot, or see the size guide in the Techniques section (page 132). The slippers are meant to stretch a little for a snug fit, so don't add anything for luck. The chart (right) shows how many stitches to cast on. Note that some sizes can be worked using different needles and/or yarn:

Slippers (make 2)

Work in garter stitch throughout.

Tip

For a completely reversible slipper, omit the insoles and make another pair in a different shade of the same yarn. Turn the second pair inside out, insert in the first pair and work the double crochet edging through the inner and outer slipper at the same time.

Shoe size chart

Approx shoe size	Approx shoe size	To fit foot length (cm)	To fit foot length (in)	Metric needle size	Sts per in/ 2.5cm	Yarn	Cast on
24–27	7–9	14–15	5½–6	3mm	6	Fine DK	22 sts
27–31	9–11	16–18	6½–7	3mm	6	Fine DK	24 sts
32–33	13–2	19–20	7½–8	3mm	6	Fine DK	26 sts
34–37	2–3	21–23	8½–9	3mm	6	Fine DK	28 sts
28–32	9–11	16.5–19	6½–7½	3.5mm	5.5	DK	22 sts
32–34	12–2	19–20	7½–8	3.5mm	5.5	DK	24 sts
34–37	2–4	21–23	8½–9	3.5mm	5.5	DK	26 sts
37–39	4–6	23–24	9–9½	3.5mm	5.5	DK	28 sts
31–33	12–2	18–20	7–8	4mm	5	Aran	22 sts
33–36	3–4	20–23	8–9	4mm	5	Aran	24 sts
37–39	4–6	23–25	9–10	4mm	5	Aran	26 sts
40–43	7–9	25–28	10–11	4mm	5	Aran	28 sts
33–34	13–3	19–21	7½–8	4.5mm	4.5	Aran	22 sts
34–37	3–4.5	21–23	8½–9	4.5mm	4.5	Aran	24 sts
38–41	5–7.5	24–25	9½–10	4.5mm	4.5	Aran	26 sts
42–44	8–10	26–29	10½–11½	4.5mm	4.5	Aran	28 sts

Sole

*Using needles indicated on the chart and leaving a long end for joining, cast on 22[24:26:28] sts.

Row 1: Knit.

Row 2 (inc): Kfb, k to last 2 sts, kfb, k1.

Row 3 (RS): Sl1, k across.

Rep last 2 rows until there are 36[40:44:48] sts on needle.

Next row: Sl1, k to end.

Next row (dec): Skpo, k to last 2 sts, k2tog.

Rep last 2 rows until there are 22[24:26:28] sts on needle.**

Upper

Next row (RS): Cast on 7[8:9:10] sts for heel at beg of row (29[32:35:38] sts), k to end.

Toe shaping

Next row: Kfb, k to end.

Next row: Sl1, k across.

Rep last 2 rows until there are 36[40:44:48] sts on needle.

Foot opening

Next row (RS): Cast off 20[22:24:26] sts, k to end (16[18:20:22] sts).

Next row: Sl1, k to end.

Rep last row 12[16:18:20] times.

Note: *For a narrow foot, work 2 fewer rows here.*

Next row (RS): Cast on 20[22:24:26] sts at beg of row, k to end (36[40:44:48] sts).

Next row: Skpo, k to last 2 sts, skpo, k to end.

Next row: K to end.

Rep last 2 rows until 29[32:35:38] sts rem.

Cast off, leaving a long yarn end for sewing up.

Inner sole (optional)

Using oddment of contrast yarn and the same needles as the slipper, work from * to **. Cast off.

Making up

Working from outside of slipper, join cast-on edge to first 28 stitches of cast-off edge, then join remaining stitches as far as the centre point of the sole. Join shaped front of toe to sole, matching centre point and easing in fullness. Turn work inside out, position inner sole, and catch stitch in place. Turn work right way out and join heel seam using mattress stitch (see page 147).

Edging

Using the crochet hook, work a row of double crochet around the top edge of the slipper. Fasten off and weave in the ends.

Adding soles

See page 134 for ideas on adding non-slip soles to the slippers.

Finishing touches

Decorate your slippers with daisy lace, motifs, fabric roses or bows. These are really easy to add: just thread a short length of ribbon through a large needle, weave through the front of your work and tie.

These simple slip-ons in cotton-look yarn are perfect for summer; they are easy to pop into your holiday luggage and into the wash. The garter-stitch sides hug the foot snugly.

Summer slip-ons

Sizes

S[M:L] to fit UK adult shoe size 4–5[5–6:7–8]

Tension

22 sts and 28 rows to 4in (10cm) measured over stocking stitch on 4mm needles. Use larger or smaller needles if necessary to obtain the correct tension.

Materials and equipment

Patons Smoothie DK, 100% acrylic (216yds/200m per 100g)

1 x 100g ball 1085 Blue

Pair of 4mm (UK8:US6) knitting needles

Darning needle

Sewing needle

Two ribbon roses (optional)

Right slipper

Beg at toe and using 4mm needles, cast on 13 sts and purl 1 row.

Row 1 (RS): K3, m1, k1, m1, k5, m1, k1, m1, k3 (17 sts).

Row 2 and every alt row: Purl.

Row 3: K4, m1, k1, m1, k7, m1, k1, m1, k4 (21 sts).

Row 5: K5, m1, k1, m1, k9, m1, k1, m1, k5 (25 sts).

Row 7: K6, m1, k1, m1, k11, m1, k1, m1, k6 (29 sts).

Row 9: K7, m1, k1, m1, k13, m1, k1, m1, k7 (33 sts).

Row 11: K8, m1, k1, m1, k15, m1, k1, m1, k8 (37 sts).

Row 13: K9, m1, k1, m1, k17, m1, k1, m1, k9 (41 sts).

Row 14: Purl.

Cont in stocking stitch without increasing until work measures 4[4½:4¾]in (10[11:12]cm) from beg, ending with a knit row.

Tip

This design has a centre seam joined using mattress stitch. If you are worried that your sewing up is not tidy enough, make a feature of the seam by working over it with blanket stitch.

Next row: K10, p21, k10.

Next row: Knit.

Next row: K10, p21, k10.

Rep last 2 rows until work measures 8[8½:9]in (20[21:22]cm) from beg.*

Next row: K10, turn.

Work 1¼in (3cm) in garter stitch on these sts.

Cast off, leaving a long end.

Rejoin yarn to rem sts.

Next row: Cast off 6 sts, k to end of row.

Next row: Cast off 16 sts, p to end (9 sts).

Heel flap

Work 1½in (4cm) in stocking stitch on these 9 sts.

Cast off.

Left slipper

Work as for right slipper to*.

Next row: Cast off 10 sts, k to end.

Next row: K10, turn.

Work 1¼in (3cm) in garter stitch on these 10 sts.

Cast off, leaving a long end.

Rejoin yarn to rem sts, cast off 6 sts, p to end.

Next row: Cast off 6 sts, k to end (9 sts).

Heel flap

Work 1½in (4cm) on these 9 sts.

Cast off, leaving a long end.

Making up

Using mattress stitch (see page 147), join centre seam of front of slipper and first three rows of garter stitch. Join the back edges of the slipper to the sides of the heel flap. Join the cast-off edges of the garter-stitch edging. Close the toe, making sure it lies flat. Attach a ribbon rose.

Adding soles

Apply puffy fabric paint (see page 135) to the underside of the slipper or use half-soles cut from chamois leather (see page 134).

These clever slippers are very stretchy so they are perfect if you want to make a gift but are unsure of the recipient's size. They are worked in the round, so there is no sewing up (hurrah!) and no seams to rub.

Magic slippers

Size
S[M: L] to fit UK adult shoe size 3–4[5–6:7–8]

Tension
S: 24 sts to 4in (10cm) in width measured over garter stitch using 3.25mm needles

M: 23 sts to 4in (10cm) in width measured over garter stitch using 3.5mm needles

L: 22 sts to 4in (10cm) in width measured over garter stitch using 3.75mm needles

Materials and equipment
Debbie Bliss Baby Cashmerino, 55% merino wool, 33% microfibre, 12% cashmere (135yds/125m per 50g)

2 x 50g balls 203 Teal

Set of four or five 3.25[3.5:3.75]mm (UK10[–:9]; US3[4:5]) double-pointed needles

Set of four or five 3[3.25:3.5]mm (UK11[10:–]; US–[3:4]) double-pointed needles

Stitch marker

Stitch holder or spare yarn

Darning needle

Special techniques

Provisional cast-on: cast on using a length of spare yarn; this is removed later and the stitches picked up to create seamless toe shaping

Short-row shaping: turn work before the end of the row to produce shaping; with garter stitch complicated wraps are not necessary

Slipper (make 2)

Using the oddment of contrast yarn and two dpns, provisionally cast on 24 sts. If you would rather not work a provisional cast-on, use cable cast-on (see page 136).

Shape toe

Row 1: Using main yarn, k.
Row 2: K22, turn.
Row 3: Sl1, k19, turn.
Row 4: Sl1, k17, turn.
Row 5: Sl1, k15, turn.
Row 6: Sl1, k13, turn.
Row 7: Sl1, k11, turn.
Row 8: Sl1, k9, turn.
Row 9: Sl1, k7, turn.
Row 10: Sl1, k5, turn.
Row 11: Sl1, k3, turn.
Row 12: Sl1, k4, turn.
Row 13: Sl1, k5, turn.
Row 14: Sl1, k7, turn.
Row 15: Sl1, k9, turn.

Row 16: Sl1, k11, turn.
Row 17: Sl1, k13, turn.
Row 18: Sl1, k15, turn.
Row 19: Sl1, k17, turn.
Row 20: Sl1, k19, turn.
Row 21: Sl1, k21, turn.
Row 22: Sl1, k22, turn.
Row 23: Knit across.

Undo the provisional cast-on, divide the 24 sts it holds between two dpns, and knit across these sts. If you used a cable cast-on, pick up and knit 24 sts from the cast-on edge, dividing them equally between two needles (48 sts).
Place marker for end of round.

Body of slipper

Work in rounds of garter stitch, noting that this is produced by working alternate rounds of knit and purl, changing at the stitch marker. The slight 'steps' where knit and purl meet will be virtually unnoticeable.

Round 1: Purl.
Round 2: Knit.
Rep these 2 rows a further 10[12:14] times, ending on a knit row.
Next row: P5, place next 14 sts on a stitch holder or length of yarn for foot opening. Turn.
Now work in rows of garter stitch thus:
Row 1: P5, k to end.
Row 2: K to last 5 sts, p5.
Rep last 2 rows 19[21: 23] times more, giving 20[22: 24] ridges from which to

pick up the edging sts. Adjust length here if required, but remember that garter stitch is very stretchy so the given number of rows should be enough for the stated size.

Shape heel

Row 1: P5, k15, turn.
Row 2: Sl1, k7, turn.
Row 3: Sl1, k8, turn..
Row 4: Sl1, k9, turn.
Row 5: Sl1, k10, turn.
Row 6: Sl1, k10, k2tog, turn.
Rep row 6 until 12 sts rem. Do not break the yarn as the edging is worked seamlessly.

Edging
First slipper

Round 1: Change to the smaller needles and knit across the 12 heel sts. *Pick up and knit 21[23:25] sts from the garter-stitch ridges down the side of the slipper, placing the last st in the 'corner' before the sts on the holder and knitting into the back of it to twist it and avoid creating a hole, k14 sts from holder, placing first st in corner, then pick up and knit 21[23:25] sts down the other side.* Place marker for end of round (68[72:76] sts).
Next round: Work in k1, p1 rib to end. Work 3 further rows in rib.
Next round: Rib 20[22:24], sl1, k2tog, psso, rib 11, k3tog, rib to end of round.

Next round: Rib to end.
Work 2 further rows of rib.
Cast off in rib.
Fasten off.

Second slipper

The inside and outside of the work should be virtually indistinguishable; for absolute perfection the garter-stitch change should run along the inside of each foot. To achieve this, turn the second slipper inside out and change to the smaller needles. Now work as for first slipper from * to *. Knit across 12 heel sts, place marker.
Complete as for first slipper.

Making up

Darn in yarn ends.

Non-slip soles

Because these slippers stretch to fit it is best not to sew on soles. To make them non-slip, apply puffy fabric paint (see page 135) to the soles following the garter-stitch lines.

These easy crocheted boots are joined to a ready-made suede moccasin sole. The pure wool yarn is snug enough to beat winter chills, and the cheerful colour should drive away the blues.

Pocahontas

Size
S[M:L] to fit UK adult shoe size 4–5[5–6.5:7–8.5]

Tension
15 sts and 19 rows to 4in (10cm) measured over double crochet using 4mm hook. Use a larger or smaller hook if necessary to obtain the correct tension.

Materials and equipment
Artesano Aran, 50% superfine alpaca, 50% Peruvian highland wool (144yds/132m per 100g)
3 × 100g skeins 5570 Fleet (2 skeins for a shorter slipper)
3.5mm (UK9:USE-4), 4mm (UK8:USG-6), 4.5mm (UK7:US7), 5mm (UK6:USH-8), 5.5mm (UK5:USI-9) and 6mm (UK4:USJ-10) crochet hooks
Oddment of contrast DK for edging/joining
Darning needle and large sewing needle
Pair of suede moccasin slipper soles with punched edges

Slipper (make 2)

Beg at toe and using 4mm hook, make 9[9:11] ch.

Row 1: 1 dc in 2nd ch from hook; dc in every ch to end (8[8:10] dc).

Row 2: 1 ch, 2 dc in first dc, 1 dc in each dc to last dc, 2 dc in last dc (10[10:12] dc).

Row 3: 1 ch, dc in each dc across.

Row 4: As row 2 but do not turn for next row (12[12:14] dc).

Row 5: 1 ch, rotate piece 90° anti-clockwise and work 1 dc in the end of each of the four rows worked. Rotate 90° again and work 1 dc in each of the 8[8:10] foundation ch. Rotate 90° again and work 1 dc in the end of each of the four rows of the other side edge (16[16:18] dc round the three sides). Turn and work back and forth along the row created round the three sides of the toe piece.

Row 6: 1 ch, 1 dc in each dc to end (16[16:18] dc).

Cont straight on these sts, work 15[17:19] rows.

Next row: 1 ch, 2 dc in first dc, 1 dc in each dc to last dc, 2 dc in last dc (18[18:20] dc).

Next row: 1 ch, dc in each dc across.

Divide for ankle

First side

Row 1: 1 ch, dc in each of first 6[6:7] dc, turn.

Row 2: 1 ch, dc2tog, dc in each dc to end (5[5:6] dc).

Work 15[17:19] rows straight.

Adjust length here if desired. Fasten off.

Second side

Miss 6 sts and rejoin yarn to next st.

Row 1: 1 ch, 1 dc in last 6[6:7] dc.

Row 2: 1 ch, 1 dc in each dc to last 2 dc, dc2tog (5[5:6] dc).

Complete to match first side.

Fasten off and join sides of heel, making sure work lies flat.*

Note: *When joining in yarn to work the leg, it may be easier to use a size smaller hook just for the first round.*

Leg section

Note: *If your leg is wider than average, change to a 5mm hook after round 6 and a 5.5mm hook to complete the leg.*

Round 1: Beg at back of heel and using 4mm hook, work 1 ch, 17[19:21] dc evenly along side, 2 dc into st before gap, 1 dc in each of 6 dc across gap, 2 dc into st after gap, 17[19:21] dc evenly along second side, join with sl st to ch (44[48:52] dc).

Round 2: 1 ch, dc into each dc to end. Join with sl st.

Round 3: 1 ch, dc in each of first 17[19:21] dc, dc2tog over next 2 sts, dc in each of next 6 dc, dc2tog over next 2 sts, dc in each dc to end. Join with sl st (42[46:50] dc).

Round 4: 1 ch, 1 dc in each dc around, join with sl st.

Round 5: 1 dc in each dc to first dec of round 3, dc2tog directly above dec, 5 dc to second dec of round 3, dc2tog above second dec, dc in each dc to end. Do not join; place next dc directly into first dc of previous row and begin to work in a spiral.

Change to 4.5mm hook and cont until work measures 6in (15cm) from beg of ankle section. Change to 5mm hook and cont until leg measures 9in (23cm) or length required. Change to 6mm hook and work a further 3in (7.5cm) for turned-down top.

Fasten off and darn in end.

Edging

Using 3.5mm hook and DK yarn, work dc evenly around lower edge, placing 1 dc in each row end. Work a second row of dc and fasten off, leaving a long end for sewing. To work a matching edging round the top of the leg, begin on WS of work and, using the contrast DK yarn double and 5mm hook, work 2 rows of dc.

Attaching the sole

Fit the completed upper over the sole, matching the centre toe to the centre front sole and the centre heel to the centre back sole. Match the centre of each side of the sole to the centre of each side of the upper; it may help to use safety pins. Knot a length of strong thread and take it through one hole from inside the slipper through the edging and down into the next hole. Move to the next hole and repeat. When you are happy with the positioning, sew in place using backstitch and contrast yarn. Fasten off, remove the tacking threads and weave in the ends.

Alternative sole fastening

Flip the slipper sole so suede part is inside. Invert the completed upper and fit the sole inside. Tack in place using strong thread. Turn RS out and attach the sole by oversewing, backstitch or blanket stitch (see pages 148 or 149) around the edge using contrast yarn. Remove the tacking thread and weave in the ends.

Advanced level sole fastening

Count the number of holes punched around sole. Work the first row of dc edging, counting the number of stitches. Increase or decrease if necessary while working the second row to produce the same number of dc as there are holes. Join contrast yarn to centre back of sole and, using a small crochet hook, work 1 tr through every hole. Join with a slip stitch. Beginning at the heel, join by working a row of dc through both the dc edging on the slipper and the treble edging on the sole at the same time. Fasten off and weave in the end.

Care instructions

Slipper sock soles can be hand-washed using mild detergent. Rinse well and squeeze out excess water. Stuff with paper or cloth and allow to dry.

Bring back memories of summer with these snazzy slippers made to look like beach shoes. The contrasting inner sole adds comfort as well as interest.

Espadrilles

Size

S[M:L] to fit UK adult shoe size 3–4[5–6:7–8]; approx foot length 8½[9½:10½]in (22[24:26]cm)

Tension

18 sts and 22 rows to 4in (10cm) measured over stocking stitch on 6mm needles. Use larger or smaller needles if necessary to obtain the correct tension.

Materials and equipment

Artesano British Wool Chunky, 100% wool
(115yds/105m per 100g)
1 × 100g skein 04 Mushroom
Oddment of chunky yarn in contrasting shade for inner sole
Pair of 6mm (UK4:US10) knitting needles
4.5mm (UK7:US7) crochet hook
Stitch holder or spare yarn
Darning needle
Two buttons

Slipper (make 2)

Upper

Beg at toe, cast on 10 sts.

Row 1: Knit.

Row 2: Purl.

Row 3: K1, m1, k8, m1, k1 (12 sts).

Row 4: Purl.

Row 5: K1, m1, k10, m1, k1 (14 sts).

Row 6: Purl.

Row 7: K1, m1, k12, m1, k1 (16 sts).

Rows 8–13: Work in stocking stitch.

Rows 14–20: Work in garter stitch (knit every row).

Row 21: K8, turn, placing rem 8 sts on holder or length of spare yarn.

Row 22: K1, p to last st, k1.

Work in stocking stitch, knitting the first and last sts of each purl row, until work measures 3½[4:4½]in (9[10:11]cm) from where sts were divided, ending on a purl row.

Next row: K1, m1, k to end (9 sts). Work 3 rows in stocking stitch, knitting first and last sts of each purl row.

Next row: K1, m1, k to end (10 sts). Cont in stocking stitch until work measures approx 8½[9½:10½]in (22[24:26]cm) from beg.

Cast off. Rejoin yarn to rem sts and complete to match, reversing position of increases.

Sole

Cast on 8 sts.

Row 1: Knit.

Row 2: K1, p to last st, k1.

Row 3: K1, m1, k6, m1, k1 (10 sts).

Row 4: K1, p to last st, k1.

Row 5: K1, m1, k8, m1, k1 (12 sts).

Row 6: K1, p to last st, k1.

Row 7: K1, m1, k10, m1, k1 (14 sts).

Cont in stocking stitch, knitting first and last sts of each purl row, until work measures approx 6½[7½:8½]in (16.5[18:21.5]cm) from beg.

Next row: K1, ssk, k8, k2tog, k1 (12 sts).

Next row: K1, p to last st, k1.

Next row: K1, ssk, k6, k2tog, k1 (10 sts).

Next row: K1, p to last st, k1.

Next row: K1, ssk, k4, k2tog, k1 (8 sts).

Next row: K1, p to last st, k1.

Next row: K1, ssk, k2, k2tog, k1 (6 sts).

Next row: K1, p to last st, k1.

Cast off, leaving a long yarn end.

Tip

Pull the yarn taut when working the first stitch of every row to ensure a tidy edge.

Inner sole

Work as for sole using contrasting yarn.

Making up

Darn in the ends on the sole pieces, tidying up the edges of the work as you go. Steam all pieces very lightly under a damp cloth to flatten the edges, taking care not to stretch them.

Place the main colour and contrast sole pieces together, RS outermost, and tack all round, one stitch in from the edge. Pin the upper in place on top of double soles and tack again. Beginning at the back of the heel and using a length of contrasting yarn, backstitch all round the sole, working through all three layers. Remove tacking threads.

Edging

Using a 4.5mm crochet hook and contrasting yarn, work a row of double crochet all around the edge of each slipper.

Adding soles

See page 134 for ideas on adding non-slip soles to the slippers.

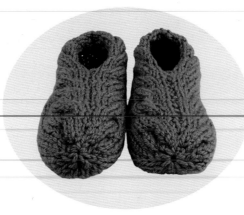

These deceptively simple slippers are the perfect opportunity to try out cables: they are based on a rectangle so there is nothing to distract you from the job in hand. All you need is a couple of spare evenings.

Chic cables

Size

To fit UK adult shoe size 3–4[5–6:7–8:9–10]

Tension

14 sts and 17 rows to 4in (10cm) measured over stocking stitch using 5.5mm needles. Use larger or smaller needles if necessary to obtain the correct tension.

Materials and equipment

Artesano British Wool Chunky, 100% wool
(115yds/105m per 100g)
1[1:2:2] × 100g skeins 02 Grey
Pair of 5.5mm (UK5:US9) knitting needles
Cable needle or double-pointed needle
Darning needle
Large sewing needle
Piece of chamois leather or synthetic chamois approx 8 × 8in
(20 × 20cm) for sole (optional)

Special abbreviations

C6B: place next three stitches on cable needle and hold at back of work, knit next three stitches, then knit stitches from cable needle.

C6F: place next three stitches on cable needle or and hold at front of work, knit next three stitches, then knit stitches from cable needle.

Slipper (make 2)

Note: This design begins at the heel.
Using 5.5mm needles cast on 36 sts, leaving a long end for sewing up.
Row 1: K9, p1, k16, p1, k9.
Row 2: K1, p8, k1, p16, k1, p8, k1.
Row 3 (cable): K2, C6B, k1, p1, k16, p1, k1, C6F, k2.
Row 4: As row 2.

Row 5: As row 1.
Row 6: As row 2.
These 6 rows form the cable pattern.
Rep 7[8:9:10] times more or number required to achieve desired length.

Tip

The cables make this design very stretchy, so the same number of stitches should fit the width of most feet. If your foot is particularly wide, just cast on two or four extra stitches and work them in as purl stitches on either side of the central stocking-stitch panel.

Shape toe

Next: K2 tog across row (18 sts).
Next: P2tog across row (9 sts).
Break off yarn leaving a long end for sewing up and thread on a darning needle. Run the yarn through the 9 rem sts and fasten off securely.

Making up

Join heel from outside, using long end left when casting on and mattress stitch (see page 147). Match sections and take care to pick up stitches from the outside edge only, so the seam lies flat and will not rub the back of the foot. At the lower end of the heel, gather the stitches slightly and ease them in carefully to avoid creating too much of a point. Join the toe for 5½[6:6½]in (14[15:16]cm), matching garter-stitch ridges carefully. Sew in all ends.

If desired, add a sole following the directions below, or apply puffy fabric paint to the bottom of your slippers to make them non-slip (see page 134).

Making a sole (optional)

Full sole: Lay slipper flat on a piece of paper and draw around it to make a template. Cut out the template about ½in (1cm) inside the drawn line.
Half sole: Make template as above. Fold in half and cut off lower section to form the sole template. Cut off about 1½in (4cm) of the upper section to form the heel template.
Lay the templates on a piece of chamois leather or synthetic chamois (see page 134). Draw around them, cut out and tack in place, or use fabric adhesive. When you are happy with the position, sew the sole in place using strong thread.

Tip

If you are worried about the back seam rubbing your heel, sew in a small piece of chamois leather across the seam or attach purchased heel grips.

These ingenious slippers look just like little purses until
you wriggle your toes into them, then they transform almost
as though by magic into a cute pair of Mary Janes.

Aran anklets

Size
S[M:L] to fit UK adult shoe size 4–5.5[5–7.5:7–8.5]

Tension
Achieving a certain tension is not crucial as these slippers are
very stretchy; just make sure you use the right size needles for
the size chosen.

Materials and equipment
Debbie Bliss Rialto Aran, 100% merino (86yds/80m per 50g)
2 × 50g balls shade 28 Terracotta
Pair of 4[4.5:5]mm (UK8[7:6]; US6[7:8]) knitting needles,
depending on size required
Darning needle
Two buttons

Slipper (make 2)

Using 4[4.5:5]mm needles, cast on 4 sts.

Row 1: Knit.

Row 2: Inc in first st, k to end.

Rep last row until there are 22 sts on the needle.

Next row: Inc in each st to end (44 sts).

Next row: K2, p2 to end.

Rep last row until work measures

5½[6:6½]in (14[15:16.5]cm).

Next row: (K2tog) across row (22 sts).

Next row: Knit to end.

Next row: K1, k2tog, k to end. Rep last row until 10 sts rem.

Next row (buttonhole): K1, k2tog, k2, yf, k2tog, k1 (7 sts).

Next row: k2tog, k5 (6 sts).

Next row: K2tog, k4 (5 sts).

Next row: K2tog, k3 (4 sts). Cast off.

Making up

Join front and back seams using mattress stitch (see page 147). Darn in ends. Attach buttons.

This close-fitting slipper in easy double crochet gets its good looks from the random yarn used. It is worked mainly in rounds so there are no seams underfoot, while the picot edging adds a pretty touch.

Random act

Size

To fit UK adult shoe size 3–4[5–6:7–8:9–10]; approx foot length 8½[9:9½:10]in (22[23:24:25]cm)

Tension

18 sts and 20 rows to 4in (10cm) measured over double crochet. Use a larger or smaller hook if necessary to obtain the correct tension.

Materials and equipment

Patons Smoothie DK, 100% acrylic (216yds/200m per 100g)
1 x 100g ball 02019 Lilac Mix
3.5mm (UK9:USE-4) crochet hook
Stitch marker
Darning needle
Sewing needle
Piece of chamois leather or synthetic chamois approx 9in (23cm) square (optional)

Slipper (make 2)

Note: *the turning chains at the beginning of rounds are not counted in the stitch total.*

Using 3.5mm hook, make a loop.

Round 1: Work 8 dc into loop, join first and last dc with sl st. Pull loop up tightly.

Round 2: 2 ch, 2 dc in each dc to end, sl st to join (16 dc).

Round 3: 2 ch, (1 dc in next dc, 2 dc in next dc); rep to end, sl st to join (24 dc).

Round 4: 2 ch, 1 dc in each dc to end, sl st to join.

Round 5: 2 ch, (1 dc in each of next 2 dc, 2 dc in next dc); rep to end, sl st to join (32 dc).

Round 6: As round 4.

Round 7: 2 ch, (1 dc in each of next 7 dc, 2 dc in next dc); rep to end, sl st to join (36 dc).

Round 8: As round 4.

Round 9: 2 ch, (1 dc in each of next 8 dc, 2 dc in next dc); rep to end, sl st to join (40 dc).

Round 10: As round 4.

Sizes 7–8 and 9–10 only

Round 11: 2 ch, (1 dc in each of next 9 dc, 2 dc in next dc); rep to end, sl st to join (44 dc).

Round 12: As round 4.

All sizes

Work in rounds of dc without increasing until slipper measures 5½[6:6½:7]in (14[15:16.5:17.5]cm) from beg or length required to cover foot to ankle.

Shape front

Next: Work 18[18:20:20] dc, dc2tog (19[19:21:21] sts). Turn.

Note: *The next row will begin at the centre front of the slipper, so the joins are hidden under the foot.*

Now work back and forth in rows.

Row 1: 2 ch, work in dc to centre back, placing dc19[19:21:21] in turning chain, then dc to within 2 sts of end of row, dc2tog (38[38:42:42] dc).

Note: *The second half of this row is actually worked 1 row down from the first half, but this will not show on the finished slippers.*

Tip

If you are making these for a man or just prefer a simple finish, work in plain dc around the foot opening.

Sizes 7–8 and 9–10 only

2 ch, miss first dc, dc to 2 dc from end, dc2tog (40 dc).

Next row: 2 ch, 1 dc in each dc to end (38[38:40:40] dc).

Rep this row until work measures 9[9½:10:10½]in (23[24:25:26]cm) or length required to reach the end of the foot.

Shape heel

Next: Sl st over next 13[13:14:14] dc, 2 ch, work 12 dc, turn.

Next row: 2 ch, work in dc to end. Work 16 rows on these central 12 dc. Fasten off, leaving a long yarn end for sewing up.

Making up

Join the side seams of the heel to the body of the slipper.

Edging

Round 1: With RS of work facing, join yarn to heel seam with a sl st and work 1 ch. Work 50 dc evenly around edge of slipper and join into a round using a sl st.

Round 2: *3 ch, miss 1 dc, 1 dc in next dc; rep from * around, sl st to join. Fasten off and darn in end.

Making a sole

Full sole: Lay slipper flat on a piece of
paper and draw around it to make a
template. Cut out the template about
½in (1cm) inside the drawn line.

Half sole: Make a template as above.
Fold in half and cut off lower section to
form the sole template. Cut off about
1½in (4cm) of the upper section to
form the heel template.

Lay the templates on a piece of
chamois leather or synthetic chamois
(see page 134). Draw around them, cut
out and tack in place, or use fabric
adhesive. When you are happy with the
position, sew the sole in place using
strong thread.

When you've danced the night away in killer heels and your feet are throbbing, you need an antidote to tortured toes. Slip a pair of these pretty pumps in your pocket and the party can go on and on.

Party pumps

Sizes

S[M:L] to fit UK adult shoe size 4–5[5–6:7–8]; approx foot length from heel to toe: 8[9:10]in (20[22.5:25]cm)

Tension

18 sts and 24 rows to 4in (10cm) measured over stocking stitch using 4mm needles. Use larger or smaller needles if necessary to obtain the correct tension.

Note: *The largest size can be worked with one ball of the specified yarn, but you may have to work the edging with an oddment of toning yarn in a similar weight.*

Materials and equipment

Bergère de France Éclair, 74% acrylic, 14% mohair, 9% wool, 3% lurex (114yds/105m per 50g) 1[1:1–2] × 50g ball(s)
63 Eclipse
Pair of 4mm (UK8:US6) knitting needles
Set of four 4mm (UK8:US6) double-pointed needles
3.5mm (UK9:USE-4) crochet hook
Stitch marker and stich holder (optional)
Darning needle and sewing needle
Sewing thread to match yarn
12in (30cm) gold organza ribbon, to finish off

Slipper (make 2)

Using 4mm straight needles, cast on 23 sts.

Row 1: Work in k1, p1 rib to end.

Row 2: Work in p1, k1 rib to end.

Rep last 2 rows until work measures 2½in (6cm).

Heel flap

Row 1: Sl1, k15, ssk, turn.

Row 2: Sl1, p9, p2tog, turn.

Row 3: Sl1, k9, ssk, turn.

Rep rows 2 and 3 until there are 11 sts on the needle.

Next row: Sl1, k8, k2tog, but do not turn (10 sts).

Shape foot

Pick up and knit 12 sts down side of heel flap, turn.

Next row: P22, pick up and purl 12 sts down other side of heel flap (34 sts). Knit straight in stocking stitch until work measures 2¾[3¼:3¾]in (7[8.25:9.5]cm) from where sts were picked up from heel flap, ending with a purl row. This will be tight for the first few rows but it will become easier.

Shape upper

Next row: K1, inc in next st, k to last 2 sts, inc in next st, k1 (36 sts).

Next row: Purl.

Next row: K1, inc in next st, k to last 2 sts, inc in next st, k1 (38 sts).

Rep last 2 rows until there are 44 sts on the needle.*

Join upper

Divide sts over 3 dpns, leaving the fourth to work with. Join into a round, twisting st at the join to avoid creating a hole. Work 1[3:5] rounds from the join, or until the slipper reaches to just under the joint of the big toe.

Next round: Knit 11 sts, then rearrange needles so first needle (N1) holds 22 sts across the front of the slipper. Knit so there are 11 sts on N2 and 11 sts on N3, ending at N4 ready for toe decreases. This will now be the start of the round, making it easier to see where to work the toe decreases. Place marker if you feel you need to.

Decrease for toe

Round 1: Ssk, k18, k2tog on N1; ssk, k9 on N2; k9, k2tog on N3 (40 sts).

Round 2: K sts on all needles without decs.

Round 3: Ssk, k16, k2tog on N1; ssk, k8 on N2; k8, k2tog on N3 (36 sts).

Round 4: K all sts without decs.

Cont thus, dec 4 sts on every alt row until 20 sts in total remain.**

Place the 5 sts from N3 on N2. Take the needles, one at a time, through to the reverse of the work, holding the points so the stitches do not slide off. Carefully turn the work inside out. There should be 10 sts on each needle, representing the top and sole of the slipper.

Join toe

Hold needles together and knit the first stitches from each together. Rep with the second stitches, then cast off the first stitch. Move on to the third stitches, k2tog and cast off another stitch. Rep to end of row. Fasten off.

Note: *If you prefer, work to ** then cast off all stitches and join the toe from the outside using mattress stitch (see page 147).*

Alternative toe (worked flat)

Work slipper to *.

Next row: P33, turn, leaving last 11 sts on a stitch holder.

Next row: K22, turn, leaving last 11 sts on a stitch holder.

Work 1[3:5] rows from division, or until slipper reaches to just under the big toe joint.

Next row: K1, ssk, k to last 3 sts, k2 tog, k1.

Next row: P to end.

Rep last 2 rows until there are 10 sts on needle. Break yarn leaving a long end and set aside.

Return to the first 11 sts you set aside. Join in yarn and purl to end of row, then purl across second group of 11 set-aside sts. Work 0[2:4] rows on these sts, or until slipper reaches to just under the big toe joint.

Complete to match sole section, then join the toe sts as above.

Join the sole section to the upper using mattress stitch (see page 147).

Edging

Using 3.5mm crochet hook and beginning at the side of the heel panel, work two rows of double crochet around the slipper, working one stitch for every two rows. Alternatively, work blanket stitch (see page 148) around the edge to finish it off.

Making up

Darn in yarn ends. Attach soles cut from chamois leather or use puffy fabric paint (see page 134). Cut ribbon in half and thread through the eye of a large needle, then take it through two or three stitches at the centre front of the slipper. Tie in a bow and trim ends.

Tip

The recommended yarn comes in 12 different shades, so you can whip up a pair to match your favourite party frock.

Chunky yarn worked on small needles produces a thick, warm fabric
that is ideal for keeping out the cold. These slippers are completely washable,
so there is no need to worry about using pale-coloured yarn.

Snow boots

Sizes

S[M:L] to fit UK adult shoe size 3–4[5–6:7–8]; approx foot
length 8½[9½:10½]in (22[24:26cm)

Tension

17 sts and 21 rows to 4in (10cm) measured over stocking
stitch using 5mm needles.
20 sts and 24 rows to 4in (10cm) measured over stocking
stitch using 4mm needles.
Use larger or smaller needles if necessary to obtain the
correct tension.

Materials and equipment

Artesano British Wool Chunky, 100% wool
(115yds/105m per 100g)
2 × 100g skeins 03 Cream
Pair of 4mm (UK8:US6) knitting needles
Pair of 4.5mm (UK7:US7) knitting needles
Pair of 5mm (UK6:UK8) knitting needles
Stitch holder or spare yarn
Stitch markers
Darning needle and sewing needle
Pair of suede slipper sock bottoms

Slipper (make 2)

Using 5mm needles and the cable cast-on method (see page 137), cast on 46[46:50] sts loosely, leaving a long yarn tail for sewing up.

Work in k1, p1 rib for 2in (5cm).

Change to 4.5mm needles and work a further 2in (5cm) rib.

Change to 4mm needles and work a further 2in (5cm) rib.

Shape heel

Rib 20[20:22] sts and turn, leaving rem sts on stitch holder or length of yarn.

Heel flap

Cont in rib for 2½[3:3]in (6.5[7.5:7.5] cm), ending with a purl row.

Instep and gussets

Next row (RS): Cast off heel sts, leaving 1 st on needle. Pick up and knit 9[9:10] sts along the inside edge of the heel flap (10[10:11] gusset sts), ssk over the first 2 sts from holder, rib across

next 21[21:23] sts from holder, k2tog, k1, cast on 9[9:10] sts for second gusset (43[43:47] sts). Mark beg and end of rib panel.

Shape gussets

Row 1(WS): P11[11:12], rib across instep sts, p to end.

Row 2: K9[9:10], k2tog, rib across instep sts, ssk, k to end (41[41:45] sts).

Row 3: P10[10:11], rib across instep sts, p to end.

Row 4: K8[8:9], k2tog, rib across instep sts, ssk, k to end (39[39:43] sts).

Row 5: P9[9:10], work across rib panel, p to end.

Cont to dec in this way until the row 'k2tog, work across rib panel, ssk' has been worked (23[23:25] sts).

Next row: P1, work across rib panel, p1.

Next row: K1, work across rib panel, k1.

Rep last 2 rows until work measures 7[7½:8]in (18[19:20]cm) from beg of gusset shaping.

Shape toe

Row 1(RS): K2, k2tog, rib to last 4 sts, ssk, k2 (21[21:23] sts).

Row 2: P3, rib to last 3 sts, p3.

Row 3: K3, k2tog, rib to last 5 sts, ssk, k3 (19[19:21] sts).

Row 4: P4, rib to last 4 sts, p4.

Row 5: K4, k2tog, knit to last 6 sts, ssk, k4 (17[17:19] sts).

Row 6: P5, rib to last 5 sts, p5.

Row 7: K5, k2tog, rib to last 7 sts, ssk,

k5 (15[15:17] sts).

Row 8: Purl.

Row 9: K5, k2tog, k1[1:3], ssk, k5
(13[13:15] sts).

Row 10: Purl.

Sizes S and M only

Row 11: K2, k2tog twice, k1, ssk twice,
k2 (9 sts)

Size L only

Row 11: K1, k2tog three times, k1, ssk
three times, k1 (9 sts).

Row 12: Purl

Row 13: Ssk, k2tog, k1, ssk, k2tog
(5 sts).
Cast off purlwise.

Making up

Sew side seam, matching heel and
gusset. Place centre of heel at back
seam of slipper sole and centre of toe
at centre front of slipper sole. Pin
evenly around and attach using blanket
stitch or by oversewing (see page 149),
using contrasting yarn if preferred.

The addition of a felt sole to this simple style worked
in chunky yarn gives a really professional finish. The foot length
is adjustable so it is suitable for a wide range of sizes.

Chunky boots

Size

S[M:L:XL] to fit UK adult shoe size 4–5[6–7:8–9:10–11]

Tension

16 sts to 4in (10cm) in width measured over stocking stitch
using 5mm needles.
14 sts to 4in (10cm) in width measured over stocking stitch
using 6mm needles.
Use larger or smaller needles if necessary to obtain the
correct tension.

Materials and equipment

Artesano British Wool Chunky, 100% wool (115yds/105m
per 100g)
2 x 100g skeins 07 Purple
Set of 5mm (UK6:US8) double-pointed needles for S–M sizes
Set of 6mm (UK4:US10) double-pointed needles for L–XL sizes
Small quantity of finer yarn for attaching soles
Darning needle and large sewing needle
Pair of ready-made leather soles or piece of leather large
enough from which to cut two soles
Hole punch if making soles

Slipper (make 2)

Using the needles recommended for the size chosen, cast on 36 sts onto one dpn, turn.

Work 1 row in 2 x 2 rib, turn.

Next row: Rib 12 sts onto the first needle; rib the next 12 sts onto a second needle; rib the next 12 sts onto a third needle. Do not turn; cont to next needle and beg to work in rounds.

Round 1: Work in rib, keeping 12 sts on each needle and using the yarn tail left when casting on as marker for beg of each round.

Rep round 1 for 4in (10cm) or length required.

Change to stocking stitch (every row knit) and work a further 6 rounds.

Shape heel

Knit 18 sts onto one needle and turn, setting aside rem 18 sts on a length of spare yarn.

Work 15 rows of stocking stitch on the 18 heel sts, ending on a knit row.

Short-row heel shaping

Row 1: Sl1p, p9, p2tog, p1, turn.
Row 2: Sl1k, k3, k2tog, k1, turn.
Row 3: Sl1p, p4, p2tog, p1, turn.
Row 4: Sl1k, k5, k2tog, k1, turn.
Row 5: Sl1p, p6, p2tog, p1, turn.
Row 6: Sl1k, k7, k2tog, k1.
Row 7: Sl1p, p8, p2tog, turn.
Row 8: Sl1k, k8, k2tog (10 sts on needle).

Shape sole

Set up the stitches to work in rounds again. Using a separate needle, pick up and knit 9 sts along the edge of the heel; this will be referred to as N1. Using a second needle, knit across the 18 sts set aside earlier; this will be referred to as N2. Using a third needle, pick up and knit 9 sts along the other

Tip

It is easier to join the work into a round if you work one row straight first.

side of the heel; this will be referred to as N3.

Next round: Knit 5 of the 10 heel sts onto N3, then slip rem 5 heel sts onto the other end of N1. There should be 14 sts on N1, 18 sts on N2 and 14 sts on N3 (46 sts in total). The round now begins at centre of the heel. Work 1 round of stocking stitch on these 46 sts.

Decrease for foot

Round 1: On N1, k to last 3 sts, k2tog, k1; on N2, k all sts for instep; on N3, k1, ssk, k to end (44 sts).

Round 2: Knit across all sts on all needles.

Rep last 2 rounds until there are 9 sts on N1 and 9 sts on N3 (36 sts).

Work foot

Cont in rounds until work measures 6[7:8:9]in (15.5[17.75:20:23]cm) or approx 2½in (6.5cm) less than required length of finished slipper.

Three-needle cast-off

Place needles side by side and take the points, one at a time, through to the inside of the work. Turn work inside out and ease the needles through to sit side by side. Pull length of yarn through. With a third needle, knit together the first stitches from each needle. Repeat, then pass the first stitch over the second to cast off. Rep to end of row.

Decrease for toe

Round 1: On N1, k to last 3 sts, k2tog, k1; on N2, k1, ssk, k to last 3 sts, k2tog, k1; on N3, k1, ssk, k to end.

Round 2: K all sts.

Cont thus until 12 sts in total rem (3 sts on N1, 6 sts on N2 and 3 sts on N3).

Join toe

K sts from N1 onto N3. You should now have 6 sts on each of 2 needles. Break yarn, leaving a long end for casting off.

Making up

Join the first row of the top of the slipper. Darn in all ends.

Attaching soles

Draw around the foot or an insole and use the outline to make a template for the soles. Cut out soles from leather and punch holes all round outside edge. Place suede side outermost and attach to bottom of slippers by oversewing (see page 149), using a length of finer yarn.

Tip

It will be easier to position the sole if you place an insole (or a cardboard copy of the sole) in the slipper first.

Variation

Use contrasting yarn to attach the soles to the slippers.

These snug unisex slipper socks knit up quickly and have a really easy-to-make heel. They fit adult sizes from dainty to yeti, and can also be worn inside boots or clogs.

Slipper socks

Sizes

S[M:L:XL] to fit UK adult shoe size 4–5[6–7:8–9:10–11]

Tension

16 sts and 20 rows to 4in (10cm) square measured over stocking stitch using 4.5mm needles.
15 sts and 19 rows measured over stocking stitch using 5mm needles.
Use larger or smaller needles if necessary to obtain the correct tension.

Materials and equipment

Artesano Aran, 50% superfine alpaca, 50% Peruvian highland wool (144yds/132m per 100g)
2 x 100g skeins 6315 Inchard
Set of five 4.5[5]mm (UK7[6]: US6[8]) double-pointed needles
Cable needle
Stitch holder (optional)
Darning needle

Special abbreviations

C8B (left sock): slip next four stitches on to a cable needle and hold at back of work; knit next four stitches, knit four stitches from cable needle.

C8F (right sock): slip next four stitches on to a cable needle and hold at front of work; knit next four stitches, knit four stitches from cable needle.

First sock

All sizes

Using the cable cast-on method (see page 136) and two 4.5[5:5:5] mm dpns, cast on 40 sts.

Row 1: (P2, k8) four times.

Divide sts evenly over four needles. These will now be referred to as N1, N2, N3 and N4.

Round 1: P2, k8 on N1; p2 k8 on N2; p2, k8 on N3; p2, k8 on N4. Rep round 1 four times.

Round 6 (cable front panel): P2, k8 on N1; p2, k8 on N2: p2, C8F on N3; p2, k8 on N4.

Rounds 7–13: As round 1.

Round 14 (cable): As round 6.

Round 15: As round 1.

Heel flap

Using N1, p2, k8 then purl the first 2 sts from N2 onto N1, turn (12 sts).

Next row: K2, p8, k2.

Leaving rem 28 sts on needles or a stitch holder and following patt as set, work 22 rows on these 12 sts. You should see 12 clear 'nubs' at the ends of the rows, which are where the gusset stitches will be picked up.

> ## Tip
> Working one row straight before joining work into a round makes everything much easier!

Shape gusset

Round 1: Using a second needle (N2), pick up and knit 12 sts along side of heel flap. Using a third needle (N3), work across 28 instep sts. Using a fourth needle (N4), pick up and knit 12 sts from other side of heel (64 sts).

Round 2: P2, k8, p2 on N1; work to last 3 sts, k2tog, k1 on N2; work across 28 instep sts keeping to patt as set on N3; k1, ssk, k to end on N4 (62 sts).
Round 3: Work without decreasing, keeping to patt as set.
Rep rounds 2 and 3 until 44 sts rem.

Foot section

Work straight until foot measures 2½in (6cm) less than length required. Stop working in patt now and cont in stocking stitch (every row knit) only.
Next round: Knit to centre of foot, then rearrange sts so there are 11 sts on each needle, beg with N1 and centre of foot.

Shape toe

Round 1: K to last 3 sts, k2tog, k1 on N1; k1, ssk, k to end on N2; k to last 3 sts, k2tog, k1 on N3; k1, ssk, k to end on N4 (40 sts).
Round 2: K all sts.
Rep rounds 1 and 2 until 16 sts rem.*

Join toe

K a further 4 sts on N4, then place top and bottom toe sts on two needles held parallel. Holding the points of the needles so the sts stay on, carefully take each needle individually to the inside of the work. Turn the sock inside out and place the needles parallel again.

Three-needle cast-off

Using a third needle, knit together one st from each needle. Rep, then cast off by lifting the first st over the second. Rep to end of row. Fasten off and darn in end.
Note: *If this seems too fiddly, just cast off all sts at *, fasten off and join the toe from the inside.*

Second sock

Work as for first sock, but work cable row thus:
Round 6 (cable front panel): P2, k8 on N1; p2, k8 on N2: p2, C8B on N3; p2, k8 on N4.

Making up

Darn in end left when casting on.

You may not be able to execute an entrechat, flex your knees in a perfect plié or achieve an arabesque, but you can dance around the house whenever you like in these dainty pink pumps.

Ballerina

Size

S[M:L] to fit UK adult shoe size 3–4[5–6:7–8]

Tension

24 sts and 32 rows to 4in (10cm) measured over stocking stitch using 3.5mm needles. Use larger or smaller needles if necessary to obtain the correct tension.

Materials and equipment

Debbie Bliss Rialto DK, 100% merino wool (114yds/105m per 50g)

2 x 50g balls 42 Pink

Pair of 3.5mm (UK–:US4) knitting needles

Set of four 3.5mm (UK–:US4) double-pointed needles

Stitch holders (optional)

Daming needle

Sewing needle

Pair of leather insoles with punched holes (optional)

Two ribbon rosebuds

Next: K14, then rearrange sts so the first needle (N1) holds 26 sts across the front of the slipper. Knit so there are 12 sts on N2 and 12 sts on N3, arriving back at N4. This makes it easier to see where to work the decreases.

Slipper (make 2)

Heel flap

Using 3.5mm needles, cast on 24 sts.

Row 1: (Sl1, k1); rep to end.

Row 2: Sl1, p to end.

Rep last two rows until work measures 2¾in (7cm).

Shape heel

Row 1: Sl1 knitwise, k15, ssk, turn.

Row 2: Sl1, p8, p2tog, turn.

Row 3: Sl1, k8, ssk, turn.

Rep rows 2 and 3 until there are 10 sts on the needle. Do not turn at end of last row; pick up and purl 15 sts from row end loops down side of heel.

Next row: K25, pick up and knit 15 sts down other side of heel (40 sts).

Tip

If the picked-up stitches down the heel look uneven or gappy, work mattress stitch (see page 147) over them to pull them in more.

Knit straight in st st, slipping first st of every row, until work measures 3[3¼:3¾]in (7.5[8.5:9.5]cm) from where sts were picked up from heel flap, ending with a purl row. This will be tight at first, so if you prefer work in rows but with sts divided over three dpns.

Shape upper

Next row: Inc in first st, k to last 2 sts, inc 1, k1.

Next row: Purl.

Rep last 2 rows until there are 50 sts on the needle.*

Join into a round

Change to dpns and knit across all sts, dividing equally between three dpns and working with the fourth. Join into a round at centre of upper.

Next: Work 3[5:8] complete rounds from join, or until the slipper reaches to just under the joint of the big toe.

Decrease for toe

Round 1: On N1: ssk, k22, k2tog; on N2, ssk, k10; on N3, k10, k2tog (46 sts).

Round 2: K sts on all needles without decs.

Round 3: On N1: ssk, k to last 2 sts, k2tog; on N2, ssk, k to end; on N3, k to last 2 sts, k2tog.

Round 4: K all sts.

Rep last 2 rows until there are 12 sts on N1 and 5 sts on each of needles 2 and 3.

Next (partial row): On N1 only: ssk, k8, k2tog. Place all rem sts on N2 without knitting them (10 sts on each needle).**

Take both needles individually through to the reverse of work, holding the ends so the stitches do not slide off. Carefully turn work inside out.

Join toe (three-needle cast-off)

Hold needles side by side and, using a third needle, knit the first sts from each together. Rep with the second sts, then cast off by lifting the first st on the working needle over the second.

Move to the next sts, knit them together and cast off again. Rep to end of row. Fasten off.

Note: *If you do not want to work this cast-off, work to **, then cast off all stitches in the usual way and join toe using mattress stitch (see page 147).*

Alternative toe (worked flat)

Work slipper to *.

Sole

Next row: K37, turn, leaving last 13 sts on a holder.
Next row: P24, turn, leaving last 13 sts on a holder.

Work 4[6:8] rows st st, or until sole reaches to just under joint of big toe.
Next row: Ssk, k to last 2 sts, k2 tog.
Next row: P to end.
Rep last 2 rows until 10 sts rem.
Cast off, and break the yarn, leaving a long end.

Sole

Return to first 13 set-aside sts, join in yarn and knit to end.
Next row: P13, then turn in the second group of 13 set-aside sts and purl across (26 sts).
Complete as for sole section (10 sts). Join upper to sole using mattress stitch (see page 147).

Edging

Using 3.5mm crochet hook and beginning at the side of the heel panel, work two rows of double crochet, working one stitch for every two rows around the slipper. Alternatively, work blanket stitch around the edge (see page 148).

Ties (optional)

Using dpns, pick up 3 sts from side of slipper and work in I-cord (see page 151) for approx 22in (56cm).

Making up

Weave in ends and attach ribbon roses. Attach ties.

Adding soles

Leather insoles with punched holes make ideal soles for these slippers (see page 134). Buy them a size smaller than the finished slipper and attach using backstitch (see page 149). Insert pretty inner soles to complete the slipper.

Variations

- Replace the I-cord ties with 3-stitch-wide garter-stitch ties, slipping the first stitch of each row, or use narrow ribbon.
- For a Mary Jane slipper, work a four-stitch-wide strap from inner instep to the outside edge of the foot, working a buttonhole 1in (2.5cm) from the end thus: sl1, yf, k2tog.

You can follow the Yellow Brick Road in these sparkly shoes inspired by *The Wizard of Oz*. The toe is worked in the round, but if you don't like working on four needles instructions for working on two are also given.

Ruby slippers

Size

S[M:L] to fit UK adult shoe size 4–5[6–7:8–9]

Tension

20 sts and 26 rows to 4in (10cm) measured over stocking stitch using 4mm needles. Use larger or smaller needles if necessary to obtain the correct tension.

Materials and equipment

Artesano Aran, 50% superfine alpaca, 50% Peruvian highland wool (144yds/132m per 100g)
1 x 100g hank 0042 Wester
Pair of 4mm (UK8:US6) knitting needles
Set of four 4mm (UK8:US6) double-pointed needles
Stitch marker and stitch holders (optional)
Darning needle
Sewing thread to match yarn
Small sewing needle
Sequin stars

Slipper (make 2)

Using 4mm straight needles, cast on 23 sts.

Row 1: Work in k1, p1 rib to end.

Row 2: Work in p1, k1 rib to end.

Rep last 2 rows until work measures 2½in (5cm).

Next row: Work in k1, p1 rib, inc 1 st at end of row (24 sts).

Heel flap

Row 1: Sl1, k15, ssk, turn.

Row 2: Sl1, p9, p2tog, turn.

Row 3: Sl1, k9, skpo, turn.

Rep rows 2 and 3 until there are 11 sts on the needle.

Next row: Sl1, p8, p2tog, but do not turn (10 sts).

Shape foot

Pick up and purl 12 sts down side of heel flap, turn.

Next row: K22, pick up and knit 12 sts down other side of heel flap (34 sts).

Work in stocking stitch until work measures 2¾[3¼:3¾]in (7.5[8:9.5]cm) from where sts were picked up from heel flap, ending with a purl row.

Shape upper

Next row: K1, inc in next st, k to last 2 sts, inc in next st, k1.

Next row: Purl.

Rep last 2 rows until there are 44 sts on the needle.*

Join upper

Divide sts over 3 dpns, leaving the fourth to work with. Join into a round, twisting st at the join to avoid creating a hole. Work 1[3:5] rounds from the join, or until the slipper reaches to just under the joint of the big toe.

Next round: Knit 11 sts, then rearrange needles so the first needle (N1) holds the 22 sts across the front of the slipper. Knit so that there are 11 sts on N2 and 11 sts on N3, ending at N4 ready to begin toe decreases. This will now be the start of the round, making it easier to see where to work the toe decreases. Place marker if you feel you need to.

Decrease for toe

Round 1: On N1: ssk, k18, k2tog; on N2: ssk, k9; on N3: k9, k2tog (40 sts in total).

Round 2: K all sts without decreasing.

Round 3: On N1: ssk, k16, k2 tog; on N2: ssk, k8; on N3: k8, k2tog (36 sts).

Round 4: K all sts without decreasing. Cont thus, decreasing 4 sts on every alt row until 20 sts in total remain.** Place the 5 sts from N3 on N2. Take the needles, one at a time, through to reverse of work, holding the points so the stitches do not slide off. Carefully turn work inside out. There should be 10 sts on each needle, representing the top and sole of the slipper.

Join toe
(three needle cast-off)

Place needles side by side and, using a third needle, knit the first stitches from each together. Rep with second stitches, then lift the first stitch over the second

to cast off. Move on to third stitches, knit together and cast off another stitch. Rep to end of row. Fasten off.

Note: *if you do not want to use this method, work to ** then cast off all stitches and join the toe from the outside using mattress stitch (see page 147).*

Alternative toe (worked flat)

Work slipper to *.

Next row: K33, turn, leaving last 11 sts on a stitch holder.

Next row: P22, turn, leaving last 11 sts on a stitch holder.

Work 1 (3:5) rows, or until the slipper reaches to just under joint of big toe.

Next row: Ssk, k to last 2 sts, k2tog.

Next row: P to end.

Rep the last 2 rows until there are 10 sts on needle. Break off yarn leaving a long end and set aside.

Return to the first 11 sts you set aside. Join in yarn and knit to end of row.

Next row: P11, then purl across second group of 11 set-aside sts.

Complete to match sole section, then join the toe stitches as above.

Join the sole section to the upper using mattress stitch (see page 147).

Edging

Using 3.5mm crochet hook and beginning at the side of the heel panel, work two rows of double crochet around the slipper, working one stitch for every two rows. Alternatively, work blanket stitch (see page 148) around the edge to finish it off.

Bow (make 2)

Using 4mm straight needles, cast on 6 sts and work 6 rows garter stitch, slipping first st of every row.

Row 7: K2tog, k2, k2tog (4 sts). Knit 1 row.

Row 9: K1, k2tog, k1 (3 sts). Knit 1 row.

Row 11: K1, inc in next st, k1 (4 sts). Knit 1 row.

Next row: Inc in first st, k2, inc in last st (6 sts).

Work 4 rows in garter stitch, slipping first st of every row.

Cast off.

Making up

Weave in ends. Attach bow to front of slipper, sewing over centre section several times to resemble a knot. Using matching sewing thread, attach sequins randomly over toe.

These chunky slippers are based on a traditional Japanese design. A combination of garter stitch, twisted rib and stocking stitch gives a really close fit and simply stylish looks.

Mountain form

Size

S[M:L] to fit UK adult shoe size 4–5[5–6:7–8]

Tension

16 sts and 20 rows to 4in (10cm) measured over stocking stitch using 5mm needles. Use larger or smaller needles if necessary to obtain the correct tension.

Materials and equipment

Artesano British Wool Chunky, 100% wool (115yds/105m per 100g)

1 × 100g skein 03 Cream

Set of four 4.5mm (UK7:US7) double-pointed needles

Set of four or five 5mm (UK6:US8) double-pointed needles

4.5mm (UK7:US7) crochet hook

Darning needle

Tip

Work the toe part of the slipper using a circular needle if preferred.

Slipper (make 2)

Using 4.5mm needles and the cable cast-on method (see page 136), cast on 9 sts.

Work 22 rows of garter stitch, slipping the first stitch of every row.

Next row: K9 onto one dpn; using a second dpn pick up and knit 12 sts from edge of work, turn.

Next row: K12 on first dpn, knit across 9 sts on second dpn; using a third dpn, pick up and knit 12 sts down edge of work, turn (33 sts).

Change to 5mm needles and work as set in garter stitch for 2¾[3:3¼]in (7[7.5:8.25]cm), ending on a WS row.

Join to work in rounds

Round 1: Knit across sts on N1, N2 and N3 but do not turn. Pick up the edge loop below the stitch just worked, and the corresponding loop below the stitch at the end of the first needle and knit these loops together to join work.

Round 2: (P1, k into back of next st) 6 times on N1, purl across 9 sts on N2, (K into back of next st, p1) 6 times, knit into back of made stitch which marks the end of the round and the centre point of the slipper (34 sts).

Round 3: (P1, k into back of next st) 6 times on N1, knit across 9 sts on N2, (K into back of next st, p1) 6 times, knit into back of made stitch which marks the end of the round and the centre point of the slipper (34 sts).

Rep last 2 rounds for 3in (7.5cm). Now work in rounds of st st, but keeping the g st sole section as set, for a further 1¼[1½:1¾]in (3[3.75:4.25] cm), or until work measures approx 1½in (3.75cm) less than desired length.

Next round: K5, k2tog, k4, skpo, garter stitch 7, k2tog, k4, ssk, k6 (30 sts).

Next round: K, keeping centre 7 sts in garter stitch.

Next round: K4, k2tog, k4, skpo, garter stitch 5, k2tog, k4, ssk, k5 (26 sts).

Next round: K, keeping centre 5 sts in garter stitch.

Next round: K3, k2tog, k4, skpo, garter stitch 3, k2tog, k4, ssk, k4 (22 sts).

Next round: K, keeping centre 3 sts in garter stitch.

Next round: K2, k2tog, k4, skpo, k1, k2tog, k4, ssk, k3 (18 sts).

Next round: Knit.

Next round: K1, k2tog, k4, k3tog, k4, ssk, k2 (14 sts).

Next round: K10, then rearrange sts across two needles so the 7 upper sts are on one needle and the 7 sole sts are on the second needle. Holding the needles parallel, slide the points inside the work and carefully turn it inside out. Slide the other end of both needles through so they lie parallel.

Three-needle cast-off

Using a third needle, knit together the first stitches from each needle. Rep, then pass the first stitch over the second to cast off. Rep to end of row.

Making up

Beginning at one side of the heel panel and using 4.5mm crochet hook, work a row of double crochet all around the edge. Darn in ends.

Adding soles

See page 134 for ideas on adding non-slip soles.

Support fair trade and keep your feet warm with these simple but effective slippers. The pure wool yarn is dyed and spun by hand in Uruguay, and each hank is signed by the artisan who produced it.

Classic boots

Size

S[M:L:XL] to fit UK adult shoe size 4–5[5.5–6.5:7–8.5:9–10.5]; approx foot length 9[9½:10½:11]in (23[24:27:28]cm)

Tension

19 sts and 38 rows to 4in (10cm) measured over garter stitch using 4.5mm needles. Use larger or smaller needles if necessary to obtain the correct tension.

Materials and equipment

Manos del Uruguay Wool Clasica Variegated 100% wool (138yds/126m per 100g) 1[1:2:2] x 100g hank 7306 Paris
Pair of 4.5mm (UK7:US7) knitting needles
Stitch holder or spare needle
Darning needle
Large sewing needle
Two large buttons

Slipper (make 2)

Toe

Cast on 18[20:22:24] sts and k1 row.

Increase for upper and sole

Next row: Sl1, inc by knitting into front and back of next st, k to end. Rep last row until there are 60[64:68:72] sts on needle.

Divide for side 1

Next row: Knit.

Next row: Sl1, skpo, knit 27[29:31:33] sts, turn, leaving rem 30[32:34:36] sts on a holder or spare needle.

Next row: Sl1, skpo, k to end. Rep last row until 2 sts rem.

Next row: K2tog and fasten off.

Side 2

Rejoin yarn to rem sts and k to end.

Next row: Sl1, skpo, k to end. Rep last row until 2 sts rem.

Next row: K2tog and fasten off.

Making up

Fold work in half down centre of V-shape. Join toe by picking up loops from the cast-on edge, making sure that the work lies as flat as possible. Join the two long edges by picking up the end loops between rows only, as this will be the seam under the foot and must lie flat. Join the back seam in the same way, easing slightly over the heel to avoid creating an obvious point.

Adding soles

See page 134 for some ideas on adding non-slip soles to the slippers. Alternatively, make paper templates, cut out crescent-shaped pieces of chamois leather for the toe and heel, attach with fabric adhesive, then sew in place. This will not prevent the garter-stitch centre section from stretching to accommodate the foot.

These really chunky slipper socks are big enough and tough enough for the man in your life. Worked in the round from the toe upwards, they grow really quickly and should last for years.

Man-size

Size

S[M:L:XL] to fit UK adult shoe size 8–9[9–10:10–11:11–12]; approx foot length 10[10½:11:11½]in (25.5[27:28:29]cm)

Tension

14 sts and 21 rows to 4in (10cm) over stocking stitch using 5mm needles and yarn held double.
13 sts and 20 rows to 4in (10cm) over stocking stitch using 5.5mm needles and yarn held double.
Use larger or smaller needles if necessary to obtain the correct tension.

Materials and equipment

Artesano Aran, 50% superfine alpaca, 50% Peruvian highland wool (144yds/132m per 100g)
2 × 100g skeins shade 8316 Deep Teal (M)
Oddments of same yarn in three different contrasting shades
Set of five × 5mm (UK6:US8) double-pointed needles for S and M sizes
Set of five × 5.5mm (UK5:US9) double-pointed needles for L and XL sizes
Stitch marker
Stitch holder or spare yarn
Darning needle

Increase for instep

Round 1: On N1 k1, M1, k to end; on N2 k to last st, M1, k1; k across all sts on N3 and N4 (34 sts).

Round 2: K across.

Rep rounds 1 and 2, inc by 2 sts every round, until there are 14 sts on N1 and N2 (44 sts total).

Place sts from N3 and N4 on a stitch holder or length of spare yarn and work across sts on N1 and N2 only.

Shape heel

Row 1: K to 7 sts from end of row, W&T.

Row 2: P to 7 sts from end of row, W&T.

Row 3: K to 9 sts from end of row, W&T.

Row 4: P to 9 sts from end of row, W&T.

Row 5: K to 11 sts from end of row, W&T.

Row 6: P to 11 sts from end of row, W&T.

Tip

You may find the heel shaping easier to work if you transfer the stitches to regular straight needles for this section only.

Special abbreviations

W&T: wrap and turn: (knitwise) yarn forward, slip next stitch to right needle, yarn back, slip stitch back to left needle, turn; (purlwise) yarn back, slip next stitch to right needle, yarn forward, slip stitch back to left needle, turn.

Slipper (make 2)

Note: *Yarn is held double throughout.*
Using two dpns and contrast yarn held double, cast on 8 sts.

Row 1: K to end.

Rotate work and, using a dpn, pick up and knit 8 sts along the cast-on edge. There will now be 8 sts on each of two needles held parallel, ready to work in rounds. This will be tight at first, but will become easier after a few rows.

Begin rounds

K 4 sts onto one dpn (N1), 4 sts onto a second (N2), 4 sts onto a third (N3) and 4 sts onto a fourth (N4).

Begin increases

Round 1: (N1) k1, M1, k to end; (N2) k to last st, M1, k1; (N3) k1, M1, k to end; (N4) k to last st, M1, k1 (20 sts).

Round 2: K around (20 sts). Mark end of round.

Rep last two rounds until there are 8 sts on each needle (32 sts total). Work 4 rounds in stocking stitch (every round knit).

Change to main shade and work in rounds without increasing until work measures 6½[7:7½:8]in (16.5[18:19:20] cm) from beg, or 3½in (9cm) less than length required.

Row 7: K to last 7 sts, skpo, turn.
Break off main colour and join in a second contrasting colour for heel.
Row 8: P15, p2tog, turn.
Row 9: K15, skpo, turn.
Cont thus until all the main colour sts have been worked off (16 contrast sts on needle).
Break off contrast yarn and place all sts back on dpns ready to work in rounds.

Work ankle

Join in main colour.
Next round: K to end (32 sts).
Rep last round for a further 3in (7.5cm).
Break off main colour and join in third contrasting shade.
Work in rib for 1½in (3.5cm).
Cast off loosely in rib.

Making up

Darn in yarn ends.

Variations

- Mix up the contrasting shades used for the toe, heel and rib sections.
- Work the slippers in a single colour (extra yarn may be needed).

If you have ever shrunk a pullover accidentally, you will enjoy this design: you have full permission to do your worst with the washing machine! If you don't like working from charts, the star pattern is also written out in full.

Felted slip-ons

Size

S[M:L] to fit UK adult shoe size 4–5[5–6:7–8]; approx foot length 9[10:11]in (23[25:28]cm)

Tension

10 sts and 21 rows to 4in (10cm) measured over garter stitch using 6.5mm needles and yarn held double. Use larger or smaller needles if necessary to obtain the correct tension.

Materials and equipment

Twilleys Freedom, 100% wool (54yds/50m per 50g)
3 x 50g balls shade 402 Black (M)
1 x 50g ball shade 434 Magenta (C)
Pair of 6.5mm (UK3:US10.5) knitting needles
Darning needle

Chart over 13 sts and 13 rows

Slipper (make 2)

Using 2 strands of black (M), cast on 9 sts.

Row 1: Knit to end.

Row 2: Inc in first st, k to last st, inc in last st (11 sts).

Row 3: K to end.

Row 4: Inc in first st, k to last st, inc in last st as row 2 (13 sts).

Work 44[50:56] rows in g-st.

Next row: Skpo, k to last 2 sts, k2tog (11 sts).

Next row: K to end.

Next row: Skpo, k to last 2 sts, k2tog (9 sts).

Cast off.

Upper

Using 1 strand of B, cast on 21 sts and work 3 rows in g st.

Change to contrast yarn (C).

Row 4: Knit.

Row 5: Purl.

M and L sizes only: Rep last two rows once. Now refer to chart to work pattern over centre 13 sts and 13 rows, stranding the yarn loosely across the back. Alternatively, follow the written instructions (right).

Pattern instructions

Row 1: K7C, 1M, 5C, 1M, k7C.

Row 2: P7C, 2M, 3C, 2M, 7C.

Row 3: K7C, 3M, 1C, 3M, 7C.

Row 4: P4C, 13M, 4C.

Row 5: K5C, 11M, 5C.

Row 6: P6C, 9M, 6C.

Row 7: K7C, 7M, 7C.

Row 8: P6C, 9M, 6C

Row 9: K5C, 11M, 5C.

Row 10: P4C, 13M, 4C.

Row 11: K7C, 3M, 1C, 3M, 7C.

Row 12: P7C, 2M, 3C, 2M, 7C.

Row 13: K7C, 1M, 5C, 1M, 7C.

Work 2[4:6] rows st st.

Next row: Skpo, k to last 2 sts, k2tog (19 sts).

Next row: P2tog, p to last 2 sts, p2tog (17 sts).

Next row: Skpo, k to last 2 sts, k2tog (15 sts).

Next row: Purl.

Cast off.

Making up

Fold sole in half and mark centre point on either side. Match the lower edge of the black top band with the centre sole markers and join. Join sides of upper from WS by oversewing (see page 149) through one or two strands at the edge of the rows to avoid creating a thick seam. Ease in fullness round the toe if necessary. Darn in all ends.

Felting

Place slippers in drum of washing machine and add a towel to provide the friction necessary for felting. Add a small amount of detergent. Run through a full cycle at 50°C (120°F). The work will shrink by approximately 30%. If the slippers are too big after the first wash, repeat the process. After washing, pull work to shape, trying on foot if possible. Stuff with paper and leave to dry.

Adding soles

It is difficult to sew soles onto thick felt. If you want to make the soles non-slip, try adding puffy fabric paint (*see page 134*), or cut out soles from leather offcuts and stick them on using fabric adhesive.

Variations

- Use oddments of felting yarn for the upper and work in stripes.
- Omit the star pattern and use an iron-on motif.

Techniques

How to create your slippers

Measuring your feet

Many of the designs in this book will stretch to fit a range of sizes, so exact measurements are not usually crucial. Remember that felted designs (such as Felted slip-ons, page 126) will be firmer and have less give, though one advantage of felting is that the slipper can be made to fit the foot exactly. These charts offer guides to average sizes.

Women's shoe sizes

UK size	US size	Metric size	Approx foot length
2	4.5	34	8½in (21.5cm)
3	5.5	35.5	8¾in (22.5cm)
4	6.5	37	9in (23cm)
5	7.5	38	9½in (24cm)
6	8.5	39	9¾in (24.5cm)
7	9.5	40	10¾in (25.5cm)
8	10.5	42	10¾in (26.5cm)

Children's shoe sizes

UK size	US size	Metric size	Approx foot length
5	5.5	21	4¾in (12cm)
6	7	23	5⅛n (13cm)
7	8	24	5½in (14cm)
8	9.5	26	6in (15cm)
9	10	27	6³⁄₁₆in (15.5cm)
10	11	28	6½in (16.5cm)
11	11.5	29	6¾in (17.5cm)
12	13	31	7in (18cm)
13	1	32	7½in (19cm)
1	2	33	8in (20cm)
2	3	34	8¼in (21cm)
3	4	36	8½in (22cm)

Men's shoe sizes

UK size	US size	Metric size	Approx foot length
4	4.5	36	8¾in (22.5cm)
5	5.5	38	9¼in (23.5cm)
6	6.5	39/39.5	9¾in (24.5cm)
7	7.5	40.5	10³⁄₁₆in (25.5cm)
8	8.5	42	10⅝in (26.5cm)
9	9.5	43	11in (27.5cm)
10	10.5	44.5	11³⁄₁₆in (28.5cm)
11	11.5	45	11½in (29.5cm)
12	12.5	46	12in (30.5cm)
13	13.5	47	12½in (31.5cm)

Before you begin

Tension

It is important to check your tension (known as 'gauge' to US knitters and crocheters), as even a small variation can make a significant difference to the size of the completed article. The pattern instructions will state how many stitches to cast on in order to produce a width of 4in (10cm). Work in stocking stitch (or the stitch stated in the pattern instructions) for 4in (10cm), then cast off and measure the finished sample.

If the tension swatch is too wide, your tension is looser than required, so try working the swatch again using smaller needles. If the swatch is too narrow, your tension is tighter than required, so try again using larger needles. When your sample measures 4in (10cm) wide, count the rows so you know how many will produce a height of 4in (10cm).

Tension squares are also important in crochet, and are produced in a similar way, beginning from a chain base.

Choosing yarn

A wide range of yarn can be used for slippers, though some fancy yarns may not be as durable or may stretch too much in wear. Natural fibres such as cotton or wool, perhaps with added synthetic fibre for strength, are usually best. It is usually possible to substitute a different yarn from that specified in the pattern, but if you decide to do this checking your tension is particularly important. For felted slippers, use only pure wool and make sure it has not been pre-shrunk or given a 'super-wash' treatment.

Needles

Many of the knitted designs in this book are made using straight needles. Take care to choose needles that are long enough to hold all the stitches comfortably, or you may find working difficult. Some designs worked in the round have also been included. For these, double-pointed needles are recommended, though a circular needle may be used if you are confident with the technique.

Hooks

These are available in materials ranging from metal and plastic to bone and bamboo. Metal hooks are smooth and durable, but other materials may be warmer to the touch. Use whichever you feel most comfortable with.

Guide to number of stitches per 4in (10cm)

Yarn Sts to 4in (10cm)	4ply	DK (light)	DK (standard)	Aran	Chunky	Super-chunky
	28	24	22	20	18–20	7–10

Adding soles

If the design you have chosen does not have integral soles, you may want to add non-slip soles. Unless every room in your home is fully carpeted, unadorned yarn slippers may be too slippery. Non-slip soles are especially important for the safety of children and older people. There are various ways to finish your slippers.

DIY soles

An economical option is to use leather offcuts – which are available from old-fashioned leather goods shops or online – or chamois leather, which can be bought in pieces from motoring supplies stores. To use, make a paper template by drawing around the finished slipper or the feet of the intended wearer and cut out using sharp scissors. Attach the sole to the slipper using fabric adhesive, then sew in place using a needle sharp enough to puncture the leather. This may also be done using a sewing machine but it can be tricky, especially for smaller sizes.

Foam insoles

Cloth-backed foam insoles produced for insertion into shoes can often be used as slipper soles. They can be cut to size using scissors and sewn in place using blanket stitch and a sharp needle.

Non-slip dots

An easy way to make soles less slippery is to use circles of felt, remembering that this may mean the slipper cannot be washed. Dots of press-fit fastening tape can also be used. Sew these on rather than using fabric adhesive for a longer-lasting result.

Ready-made soles

Many different types of ready-made soles are available from good craft shops or online. These include leather or suede soles designed to attach to the bottom of the slipper. This type of sole often has small holes punched round the edge so they can be attached by oversewing or blanket stitch (see page 148).

Another type available is a washable suede moccasin base that comes complete with furry lining. The advantage of this is that only the upper needs to be made, and is then joined to the moccasin sole using the holes punched around the edge.

If you do use ready-made soles, make sure they are exactly the right size for the foot of the wearer or you may spoil the look of your slipper. Most types can be trimmed to size.

Lining
To make your slippers even warmer, you could line them with purchased insoles, foam rubber cut to fit, or offcuts of sheepskin or fake fur. You may like to secure linings using fabric adhesive or by stitching.

Puffy fabric paint

An innovative way to add non-slip properties to a pair of slippers is with puffy fabric paint. Apply the paint to the underside of the finished slipper using dots, circles or squiggly lines and allow to dry thoroughly. This type of paint is available from craft shops or online retailers, and video instructions on its use can be viewed online. Note that this method is best suited for slippers that will have light use, as the paint can rub off.

Knitting techniques

Simple cast-on

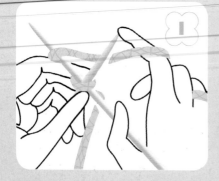  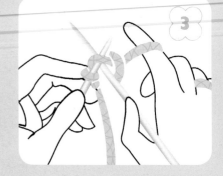

1 Form a slip knot on the left needle. Insert the right needle into the loop and wrap yarn around it as shown.

2 Pull the yarn through the first loop to create a new one.

3 Slide it onto the left-hand needle. There are now two stitches on the left needle. Continue in this way until you have the required number of stitches.

Cable cast-on

1 For a firmer edge, cast on the first two stitches as shown (right).

2 When casting on the third and subsequent stitches, insert the needle between the cast-on sts on the left needle, wrap the yarn around and pull through to create a loop. Slide the loop on to the left needle. Repeat to end.

 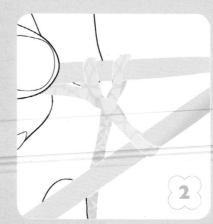

Thumb method cast-on

1 Make a slip knot some way from the end of the yarn and place on the needle. Pull the knot tight.

2 Hold the needle in your right hand and wrap the loose tail end around the left thumb, from front to back. Push the needle point through the thumb loop from front to back. Wind the ball end of yarn around the needle from left to right.

3 Pull the loop through the thumb loop, then remove your thumb. Gently pull the new loop tight using the tail yarn. Repeat until the desired number of stitches are on the needle.

Casting off

1 Knit two stitches onto the right needle, then slip the first stitch over the second stitch and let it drop off the needle (one stitch remains).

2 Knit another stitch so you have two stitches on the right needle again. Repeat the process until there is only one stitch on the left needle. Break the yarn and thread through the remaining stitch to fasten off.

Knit stitch (k)

1 Hold the needle with the cast-on stitches in your left hand. Place the tip of the empty right needle into the first stitch and wrap the yarn around as for casting on.

2 Pull the yarn through to create a new loop.

3 Slip the newly made stitch onto the right needle.

Purl stitch (p)

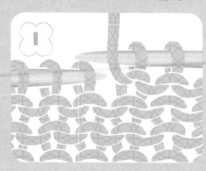

1 Hold the yarn at the front of the work as shown.

2 Place the right needle into the first stitch from front to back. Wrap the yarn around the needle in an anti-clockwise direction as shown.

3 Bring the needle back through the stitch and pull through. Continue in the same way for each stitch on the left-hand needle. To start a new row, turn the work to swap the needles around and repeat the steps.

Shaping knitted pieces

Many of the slipper patterns feature shaping by increasing or decreasing stitches to ensure a good fit. The following techniques are featured in this book.

Increases

Kfb: knit into the front and back of the next stitch (increase by one stitch).

M1: make one stitch (increase by one stitch) by picking up the loop between the stitch on the needle and the next stitch and knitting it.

M1p: make one stitch (increase by one stitch) by picking up the loop between the stitch on the needle and the next stitch and purling it.

Decreases

K2tog: insert RH needle into front of next two stitches and knit them together (decrease by one stitch).

P2tog: insert RH needle from right to left into front of the next two stitches and purl them together (decrease by one stitch).

Skpo: slip one stitch from LH to RH needle, knit the next stitch, pass the slipped stitch over the knitted stitch (decrease by one stitch).

Ssk: slip the next two stitches knitwise, one at a time, then insert the left needle into the front of these stitches from left to right and knit them together through the back loops (decrease by one stitch).

Sssk: work as for ssk, but slip and knit together three stitches to decrease by two stitches.

Stitch variations

A Garter stitch (g st)

Knit every row.

B Stocking stitch (st st)

Knit on RS rows and purl on WS rows.

C Moss stitch (m st)

With an even number of stitches:
Row 1: (K1, p1) to end.
Row 2: (P1, k1) to end.
Rep rows 1 and 2 for pattern.

With an odd number of stitches:
Row 1: * K1, p1; rep from * to last stitch, k1.
Rep to form pattern.

D Single (1 x 1) rib

With an even number of stitches:
Row 1: *K1, p1; * rep to end.
Rep for each row.

With an odd number of stitches:
Row 1: *K1, p1, rep from * to last stitch, k1.
Row 2: *P1, k1, rep from * to last stitch, p1.

E Double (2 x 2) rib

Row 1: *K2, p2; rep from * to end.
Rep for each row.

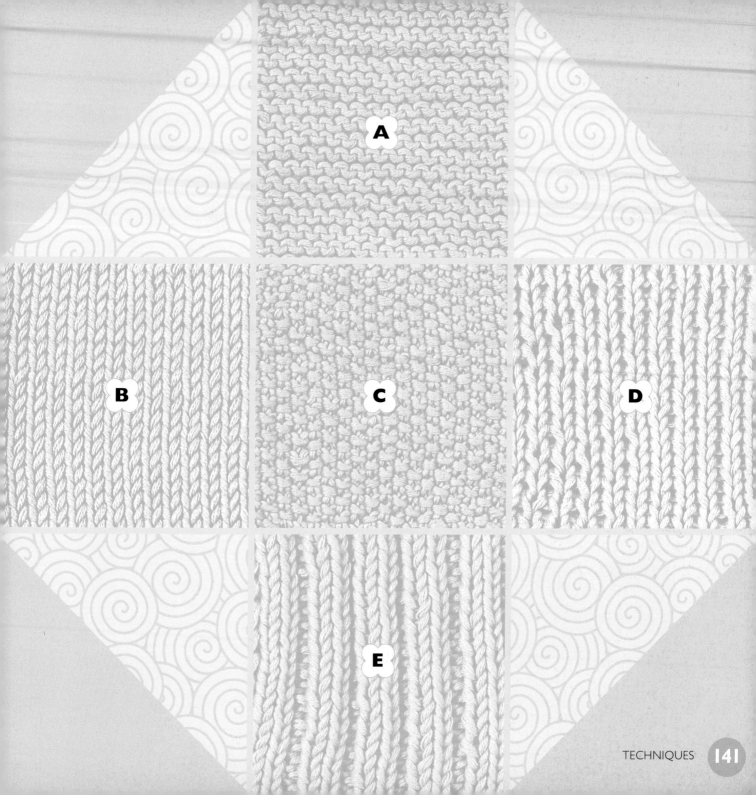

Cable stitch

With the help of a cable needle (this is a short double-pointed needle with a kink in it to hold stitches), these decorative stitches are quite straightforward to make. Stitches are slipped onto the needle and then knitted later to create the twists in the fabric. If you don't have a cable needle, use a double-pointed needle instead.

Front cable worked over 4 stitches (C4F)

1 Slip the next two stitches onto a cable needle and hold in front of the work.

2 Knit the next two stitches from the left needle as normal, then knit the two stitches from the cable needle.

Back cable worked over 4 stitches (C4B)

Slip the next two stitches onto a cable needle and hold at back of the work.

Knit the next two stitches from the left needle as normal, then knit the two stitches from the cable needle.

Knitting in the round

Many knitters are not confident enough to try working in the round, but it is quite easy once you have mastered the basics. It is also the fastest way to knit: there are no seams to join, and the right side of the work is always facing, so working patterns becomes easier.

Tip

To avoid the dreaded 'ladder' effect that can occur when working in the round, rearrange the stitches on the needles every few rounds to move the stress points. One way to do this is by working two extra stitches from the next needle. Take care to mark the beginning of the actual round, or you will find it hard to tell where it technically began.

Working with double-pointed needles

Double-pointed needles (dpns) usually come in sets of four or five. Reserve one needle to work with and space the cast-on stitches evenly over the remaining needles.

1 Cast on the required number of stitches, divided equally over three needles. Lay the work flat to check that it is not twisted.

2 Insert a fourth needle (the working needle) into the first stitch on needle 3 (N3), and knit the stitch. The yarn will be coming from the last stitch on N1, so working the first stitch will join the work. Pull the first few stitches tighter than in normal knitting to keep the join snug and avoid gaps between stitches. Then simply work the stitches from each needle as you come to them, round and round.

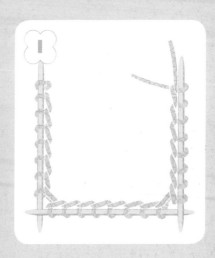

Crochet techniques

Chain stitch (ch)

1 With the hook in your right hand and the yarn resting over the middle finger of your left hand, pull the yarn taut. Take the hook under, then over the yarn.

2 Pull the hook and yarn through the loop while holding the slip knot steady. Repeat to form a foundation row of chain stitch (ch).

Slip stitch (sl st)

1 Insert the crochet hook into the stop of the next stitch and wrap the yarn around the hook.

2 Use the hook to draw the yarn back through the top of the stitch and the loop on the hook.

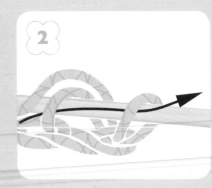

Double crochet (dc)

1 Place hook into a stitch. Wrap the yarn around the hook and draw the loop back through the work towards you.

2 There should now be two loops on the hook. Wrap the yarn around the hook again, then draw through both loops, leaving one loop on the hook. One double crochet (dc) stitch is now complete. Repeat to continue row.

Tips

Chain stitch is the usual base for other crochet stitches and is also useful for making simple ties. Double crochet produces a dense fabric that is ideal for lining, while single rows are ideal for edging. Crochet worked in half treble and treble stitch has a more open weave.

Half-treble (htr)

Wrap the yarn around the hook, then insert into a stitch. Wrap the yarn around the hook, then draw the loop through (three loops now on hook). Wrap the yarn around the hook again and draw through the three loops (one loop remains on the hook).

Treble (tr)

Follow the instructions for half treble until there are three loops on the hook. Catch the yarn with the hook and draw through two of the loops, then catch the yarn again and draw through the remaining two loops.

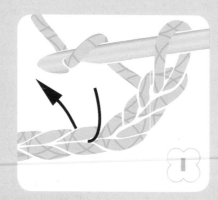 

Shaping crochet pieces

As with the knitted patterns, some of the crochet slippers are shaped by increasing or decreasing. To increase, work more than once into the same stictch.

Dc2tog: double crochet two stitches together to decrease: (insert hook into next stitch and draw up a loop) twice [three loops on hook]; (yarn over hook and draw through two loops) twice.

Sewing up

Mattress stitch

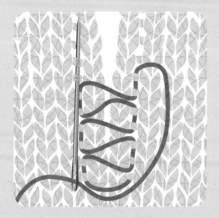

Join pieces from the right side of the work. Using matching yarn, weave the needle back and forth, taking small straight stitches. The stitches will form a 'ladder' between the two pieces of fabric to create a flat seam. This technique can also be used to join crochet pieces.

Garter-stitch joins

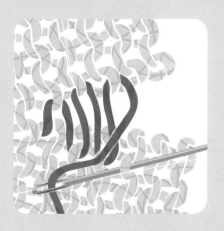

It is easy to join garter stitch as it has a firm edge and lies flat. Place the edges of the work together, right side up, and see where the stitches line up. Pick up the bottom loops of the stitches on one side of the work and the top loops of the stitches on the other side.

After a few stitches, pull gently on the yarn. The stitches should lock together and lie completely flat. The inside of the join should look the same as it does on the outside.

Attaching soles

Blanket stitch, running stitch, backstitch and oversewing can all be used to attach soles to your slippers.

Use whichever method you prefer, but choose a durable yarn or thread so the soles will last longer.

Blanket stitch

Work from left to right. The twisted edge should lie on the outer edge of the fabric to form a raised line. Bring needle up at point **A**, down at **B** and up at **C** with thread looped under the needle. Pull through. Take care to tighten the stitches equally. Repeat to the right. Fasten the last loop by taking a small stitch along the lower line.

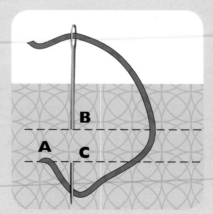

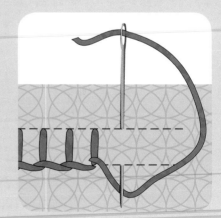

Running stitch

Bring the needle out to the right side of the work. Push the needle in and out of the work. Repeat at regular intervals, aiming to make each stitch and each gap between stitches the same length.

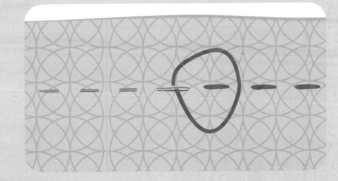

Backstitch

Make a knot to secure yarn at back of work. Bring the needle up to point A, insert at point B, and bring back up at point C. Repeat, keeping the stitches an even length.

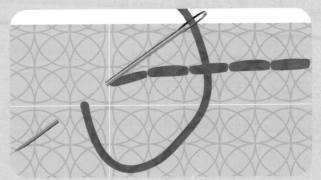

Oversewing

With wrong sides of work together, insert the needle from back to front through both pieces, slanting the needle from right to left. Pull through. Insert the needle from the back, just behind where the thread is emerging and, slanting the needle as before, bring it through to the front.

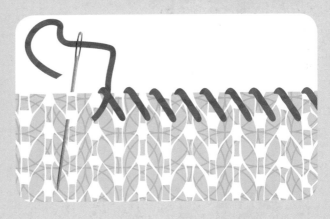

Felting knitted fabric

Felting produces a thick, durable fabric that is ideal for slippers. It is important to remember that only untreated 100% pure wool yarn should be used; avoid yarn that is mixed with other fibres, treated or described as 'super-wash', as these yarns will be resistant to the felting process. Many different types of pure wool yarn will felt successfully; if in doubt, work and wash a sample piece to check before trying out a finished article. It is also possible to buy special felting yarn and follow the manufacturer's instructions.

As a guideline, knitted fabric will shrink by about 30% when felted, so before felting your slippers may look enormous. If your work does not shrink enough on first felting, simply repeat the process until you achieve the desired result.

How to felt

Make sure there are no loose ends of yarn. Place the work in a nylon mesh bag or an old pillowcase. Place in the drum of the washing machine, adding a pair of jeans or a bath towel to produce the friction necessary for felting. Add a small quantity of washing powder and run through a full cycle at 50°C (120°F). Remove from the machine and pull gently into shape, separating the sides if necessary. Allow the slippers to dry naturally. If you have made them for yourself, try them on while damp so the felted fabric will mould to the shape of your feet. The work should felt sufficiently with just one wash cycle, but can be felted again to shrink it further.

Finishing touches

Making pompons

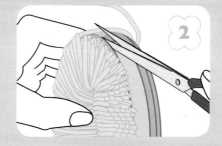
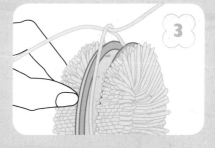

1 Cut two cardboard circles a little smaller in diameter than the pompon you want. Make a hole in the middle of both about a third of the diameter. Place both circles together and thread lengths of yarn through the middle and around the outer edge until card is completely covered and the centre hole is only a pinprick.

2 With sharp scissors, cut all around the edge of the circle, slicing through all the strands of yarn.

3 Ease a length of yarn between the card discs and tie very firmly around the centre, leaving a tail for sewing. Ease the card discs away from the pompon and fluff out all the strands. Trim off loose or straggly ends.

Making an I-cord

Using double-pointed needles, cast on the required number of stitches. Do not turn; slide stiches to the opposite end of the needle, then take the yarn firmly across the back of work. Knit stitches again. Repeat to desired length. Cast off.

Tip
Customize your slippers in any way that you like by adding motifs, pretty buttons or embroidery.

Abbreviations

alt	alternate	**kfb**	knit into the front and back of the next stitch (increase by one stitch)	**sl**	slip
beg	beginning			**sl st**	slip stitch
C4B	cable four back (or as many stitches indicated in pattern)	**LH**	left hand (needle)	**ssk**	slip the next two stitches knitwise, one at a time, then insert the left needle into the front of these stitches from left to right and knit them together through the back loops (decrease by one stitch)
		M1	make one stitch (increase by one stitch) by picking up the loop between stitch on needle and next stitch and knitting it		
C4F	cable four front (or as many stitches indicated in pattern)				
		M1p	make one stitch (increase by one stitch) by picking up the loop between stitch on needle and next stitch and purling it		
C	contrast colour			**sssk**	slip the next three stitches knitwise, one at a time, then insert the left needle into the front of these stitches from left to right and knit them together through the back loops (decrease by two stitches)
ch	chain				
cm	centimetre(s)				
cont	continue	**M**	main colour		
dc	double crochet	**mm**	millimetre(s)		
dc2tog	double crochet two stitches together (decrease by one stitch)	**p**	purl	**st(s)**	stitch(es)
		p2tog	insert RH needle from right to left into next two stitches and purl them together (decrease by one stitch)	**st st**	stocking stitch
				tbl	through back loop(s)
dec	decrease			**tr**	treble
DK	double knitting			**WS**	wrong side
dpn	double-pointed needle(s)	**patt**	pattern	**yb**	yarn back
g	gram(s)	**psso**	pass the slipped stitch over	**yf**	yarn forward
g st	garter stitch	**rem**	remain/ing	*****	work instructions following *, then repeat as directed
htr	half treble	**rep**	repeat		
in	inch(es)	**RH**	right hand (needle)	**( )**	repeat instructions inside brackets as directed
inc	increase	**RS**	right side		
k	knit	**skpo**	slip one stitch, knit the next stitch, pass the slipped stitch over (decrease by one stitch)		
k2tog	knit two stitches together (decrease by one stitch)				

Conversions

Needle sizes

UK	Metric	US
11	3mm	–
10	3.25mm	3
–	3.5mm	4
9	3.75mm	5
8	4mm	6
7	4.5mm	7
6	5mm	8
5	5.5mm	9
4	6mm	10
3	6.5mm	10.5
2	7mm	10.5

UK/US yarn weights

UK	US
4-ply	Sport
DK	Light worsted
Aran	Fingering/worsted
Chunky	Bulky
Super chunky	Extra bulky

UK/US crochet terms

UK	US
Double crochet (dc)	Single crochet (sc)
Half treble (htr)	Half double crochet (hdc)
Treble crochet (tr)	Double crochet (dc)

Crochet hook sizes

UK	Metric	US
10	3.25mm	D/3
9	3.5mm	E/4
8	4mm	G/6
7	4.5mm	7
6	5mm	H/8
5	5.5mm	I/9
4	6mm	J/10

About the author

Alison Howard has been knitting since she was nine years old. A former journalist, she worked as a magazine editor before becoming a book editor. She now works mainly as a freelance editor in the craft sector, as well as editing and checking knitting and crochet patterns, and proofreading and editing academic theses. Alison has edited books in GMC's Cozy series, has written *Mug Hugs* and co-authored *Tea Cozies 3*. She has also been a consultant or written under a 'house' name for various other titles, including *Your Tudor Homework Helper*, *Your Victorian Homework Helper*, *Extreme Machines* and *Amazing Inventions*.

Acknowledgments

GMC Publications would like to thank the following: Rebecca Mothersole and Amelia Holmwood for photographic styling and modelling; The Lamb of Lewes, East Sussex, for letting us photograph by their fireplace.

Suppliers

Artesano Ltd

Unit G, Lambs Farm
Business Park
Basingstoke Road
Swallowfield
Reading
Berkshire
RG7 1PQ
Tel: +44 (0)118 9503350
www.artesanoyarns.co.uk

Coats Crafts UK

Green Lane Mill
Holmfirth
West Yorkshire
HD9 2DX
Tel: +44 (0)1484 681881
www.coatscrafts.co.uk

Debbie Bliss

Designer Yarns Ltd
Unit 8–10
Newbridge Industrial Estate
Pitt Street
Keighley
West Yorkshire
BD21 4PQ
Tel: +44 (0)1535 664222
www.designeryarns.uk.com

Sirdar Spinning Ltd

Flanshaw Lane
Wakefield
West Yorkshire
WF2 9ND
Tel: +44 (0)1924 371501
www.sirdar.co.uk

Index

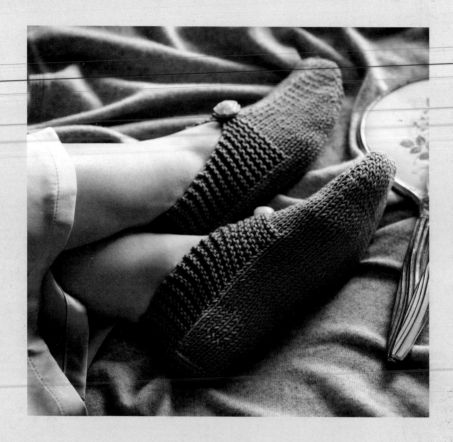

To place an order, or to request a catalogue, contact:

GMC Publications Ltd

Castle Place, 166 High Street, Lewes, East Sussex, BN7 1XU

United Kingdom

Tel: +44 (0)1273 488005

Website: www.gmcbooks.com